This book includes:

For the beginning player: A simplified winning system based on millions of hands of computer-played blackjack.

For the intermediate player: A step-by-step approach to becoming an advanced player based on an analysis of nearly a hundred blackjack systems.

For the advanced player: A recommendation for a professional system that will **maxi**mize your winnings.

D0878859

Blackjack

A Winner's Handbook

Revised and Expanded Edition

By

Jerry L. Patterson

A Perigee Book

Perigee Books
are published by
G. P. Putnam's Sons
200 Madison Avenue
New York, New York 10016

Library of Congress Cataloging in Publication Data

Patterson, Jerry L.
   Blackjack, a winner's handbook.

Bibliography: p.
   1. Blackjack (Game)   I. Title
GV1295.B55P37   1982   795.4'2   81-15404
ISBN 0-399-50616-0   AACR2

Book design by Constance Sohodski

Printed in the United States of America

Third Impression

This book is dedicated to my wife, Nancy, who was the inspiration behind its writing. Nancy worked with me throughout the writing and publication of the book. Without her continuous assistance, it would not have become a reality.

I am indebted to Walter Jaye for doing the research, analysis, and rewriting that led to the publication of this revised and expanded edition.

And Bob: This book is much more real to me because of your impressive abilities to use the data it contains to instruct our students in how to use the data. I derive just as much satisfaction out of your success and from the success of our 2000+ students as I do from my own.

Acknowledgments

Of the many persons contributing to the development of the blackjack technology described herein, two deserve special mention. Edward O. Thorp started it all with his analysis of the game that culminated with the publication of his book *Beat the Dealer*. Julian Braun continued the work over the years, and without his scholarly analyses, few, if any, of the systems reviewed herein could have been developed, the author's included.

Four persons provided me with excellent critiques of the initial draft of this book, for which I am extremely appreciative. They are Dave Fedor, Fred Gasser, Leroy Milman, M.D., and Joe Staszak. Their valuable comments had a major impact on my creative process and on the structure and content of the book.

Ruth Davis is acknowledged for the many nights she

spent away from her family typing the drafts and the final manuscript. Her valuable suggestions concerning type fonts and exhibit formats contributed greatly to the appearance of the book.

Patty Uffelman did an outstanding job of editing the final manuscript. Her valuable service significantly enhanced the readability of the book.

I would also like to thank Lyn Cohen for her many valuable comments from the perspective of a professional public relations person.

Thanks again to Don Schlesinger for a super job of technical editing.

Why Should You Buy This Book?

With the increased national popularity of gambling in the past three years, blackjack information has more than doubled. In 1977 there were fifty different blackjack systems. Now there are more than one hundred. Instead of twenty-five blackjack books, we now have over fifty. Newsletters have increased from two to nine, magazines from three to eleven, and blackjack schools from two to an even dozen at last count.

The aspiring blackjack player has twice as much material to wade through in search of an ideal system, and unfortunately the mediocre as well as the worthless information has proliferated at a rate far greater than has the really worthwhile. Much more is known about winning at blackjack than ever before, but the truly significant material is increasingly more difficult to find in the maze of blackjack data.

Blackjack: A Winner's Handbook sifts through all this information, classifies and evaluates it, and finally charts a course for the budding student of the game that will take him to any level of expertise he chooses. The recommended material amounts to less than 5 percent of the data available and should cost less than the average serious player spends on obsolete or worthless information before he finally finds something of value.

What This Book Will Do for You

1. Assist the non-system blackjack player to eliminate the casino advantage of 6 percent.
2. Explain why and how it is possible to win money playing casino blackjack.
3. Provide the occasional gambler a simplified winning strategy that can be learned in about two hours.
4. Using an analysis and comparison of nearly a hundred published blackjack systems, assist the basic player to become an intermediate and then an advanced blackjack player. A detailed step-by-step approach is presented.
5. Aid you to overcome the barriers to making big money playing blackjack.
6. Clarify the mechanics of blackjack systems.
7. Show you which blackjack systems to avoid.

8. Help you select winning basic, intermediate, and advanced blackjack systems.

9. Show you how to avoid being detected by the casinos as a system player.

10. Recommend a blackjack player's library.

11. Provide a complete index of all the reviewed blackjack systems and strategies.

Foreword—
Why This Book Was Written

Most people do not know that the casino game of blackjack can be beaten. A mathematical solution to the game was discovered in 1961. Since that time, scores of blackjack systems have been developed, many of them resulting from extensive computer studies of the game.

This book was written to satisfy the needs of the occasional gambler as he confronts these myriad systems and the large body of scientific research about the game. The book helps the occasional gambler to select the blackjack system that he is capable of learning and that best suits his style of play, the time he wishes to invest, and the risk he wishes to take.

Many occasional players have another need that may

not be satisfied by any prior blackjack book or system. They need a simple but effective blackjack system that can be learned quickly, perhaps in two hours or less. The High-Count System, developed by the author and published here, takes advantage of powerful blackjack techniques developed through hundreds of hours of computerized play, but simplifies these techniques to a method that can be learned by the average person in about two hours. High-Count utilizes a simplified basic playing strategy that is learned in accordance with the frequency of occurrences. The system is expressed by a few simple rules, not a complicated decision table. Properly applied, High-Count will increase the average non-system player's expectation of −6 percent to better than an even game: a winning expectation.

What is the attraction of playing casino blackjack? You can win! You can take money from the house! That's the fun. You can beat the dealer. That's the challenge. However, many blackjack systems take the fun out of the game. They are difficult to learn, complicated to use, and contain too many variables to remember. High-Count was developed to put the fun back into the game of blackjack.

Until the publication of this book, there was not a systematic or unbiased review of the entire blackjack systems field available anywhere. Most books have been written by skilled blackjack players from an expert's viewpoint, not from the viewpoint of the average gambler.

The author of this book, possessing technical background in mathematics and computers, interprets what these experts are saying, while maintaining the perspective of the average gambler. Twenty years of casual but consistently profitable play uniquely qualify the author to review the blackjack systems field.

For the occasional player who wants to progress to more advanced levels of play, a step-by-step approach is presented. This singular approach resulted from the author's review and analysis of nearly a hundred published blackjack systems. The recommended systems and tools are available in published books, all of which can be acquired for less than one hundred dollars.

Finally, the book was written to fill certain gaps in other blackjack publications. It presents a comprehensive glossary of terms for the beginner. It describes the "true count" in terms understandable by a layman. And most important, it presents the first realistic estimate of what the player can expect to win in a given time period.

Like any game of chance, there are risks involved in blackjack. The author cannot assume the responsibility for any losses incurred, nor does he expect any remuneration for success as a result of applying any of the systems that have been described in this book or elsewhere, published or unpublished.

FOREWORD TO
REVISED AND EXPANDED
EDITION

Reader response to the first three printings of this book has been extremely gratifying. I have received literally hundreds of letters and phone calls from blackjack players throughout the country complimenting me on this book and thanking me for fulfilling a need that has long been unmet—a blackjack book for the occasional player that takes a critical look at the entire blackjack systems field.

I am pleased to say this new edition contains an update of those books and systems that have appeared on the scene since this book was first published in 1977.

Jerry L. Patterson
December 1, 1981

CONTENTS

Part I
Background Information

Part II
A Winning Strategy
for the Occasional Player

PART III
A REVIEW AND ANALYSIS
of INTERMEDIATE AND ADVANCED
WINNING STRATEGIES

PART IV
RECOMMENDEd SOURCES of
CASINO GAMINÇ SERVICES

List of Exhibits

Introduction

It is a fact that, of all the casino gambling games, only blackjack ("21") can be beaten consistently. It has been proven mathematically that by following a simple set of decision rules that are dependent upon the dealer's up card and the player's two cards, the player can achieve an even break against the casino. Further, it has been proven that by counting those cards that have been played, the blackjack player can achieve a mathematical superiority against the casino.

Most occasional gamblers are unaware of the tremendous amount of research that has been done to provide blackjack players with winning strategies. This research has been performed, with the aid of high-speed computers, by some of the best mathematical minds in the country. Most of these researchers have used their results to make thousands—in some cases, hundreds of thousands—of dollars in the Nevada casinos. The casinos, to protect themselves, have barred many of these individuals from play. Many of the researchers, and some of those who have used their systems successfully, have written books describing these systems. Others market systems through the mail. The student of the game is confronted with fifty or more books and well over a hundred blackjack systems from which he must choose.

Recognizing this dilemma, and having a working familiarity with most of the blackjack systems, I wrote this book to aid the occasional gambler in making his choice. With the opening of the Atlantic City casinos, many persons without a working knowledge of the game will be searching for data. This book will help them sift through the available data and choose a winning blackjack strategy that is suitable to their style of play, the risks they wish to take, and the amount of time they wish to invest.

The book is divided into four parts. Part I presents background information about the game; it is preceded by a complete Glossary of Terms. Part II is dedicated to the beginning player and the occasional player. The basic blackjack playing strategy and simple card-counting systems are reviewed. The reader is shown which systems to avoid. Finally, a simple but powerful winning strategy is described, which can be learned by the average person in about two hours.

Part III of the book is written for the occasional player or intermediate player who is a serious student of the game and whose objective is to become an advanced blackjack player. Point-count systems and advanced blackjack systems are reviewed and analyzed. Recommended systems are incorporated into a step-by-step approach for becoming an advanced player. The reader is given advice on the practical aspects of casino play and introduced to the big names on the blackjack scene.

Part IV contains recommendations and endorsements for blackjack books, magazines, newsletters, and learning tools as well as blackjack schools. A complete line of casino gaming services offered by Jerry L. Patterson is listed and described.

All blackjack systems that were reviewed in conjunction with the writing of this book are listed with recommendations in the Appendix. All blackjack books known to me are listed in the Bibliography.

Glossary of Terms

This glossary is presented in logical, not alphabetical order. Reading it should give the novice a thorough understanding of the game of blackjack. The definitions apply to the casino game of blackjack.

(1) *Blackjack*

A card game played between a dealer and one to seven players. Cards are dealt in succession with each player receiving two cards. One of the dealer's two cards is exposed. The value of each hand is determined by adding the values of the two cards. Face cards count 10 and all other cards count their face value (i.e., 5 counts as 5), except ace, which counts as either 1 or 11, at the player's option. The object of the game is to beat the dealer while not going over 21 (breaking). Following the initial deal of two cards, each player, in turn, is permitted to draw as many cards as he wishes. If a player breaks (goes over 21), he immediately loses his bet. After all the players have drawn cards, the dealer turns over his unexposed card and draws cards as long as he has 16 or less. If the dealer's hand totals 17 or more, he cannot draw another card.

Blackjack also refers to a "natural" 21: the combination of an ace and a 10 or face card, dealt on the first two cards. The player is immediately paid at three to two unless the dealer also has a blackjack.

(2) *Hard Hand*   Any hand that totals 12 or more without an ace (or with an ace valued as 1).

(3) *Soft Hand*   Any hand containing an ace that totals 21 or less with the ace valued as 11.

(4) *Hit*	The player's decision to take another card. He may do this as long as he does not have 21. Most players, however, never hit a hand 17 or higher.
(5) *Dealer*	A casino employee who deals the game of blackjack. The dealer plays according to a predetermined set of rules. He must hit all his hands that total 16 or less. He may or may not hit a soft 17 depending on the casino. He plays against each player in succession and settles all bets at the end of a round of play.
(6) *Bet*	The amount of money wagered by a player that he can beat the dealer, usually between $2 and $500. The casino may set a maximum bet.
(7) *Chip* (check)	A token used in lieu of money to make the bets. A $5 chip is worth $5. Chips are color coded and marked by the issuing casino.
(8) *Rank*	The defined value of each card. The 9 of clubs has a rank of 9. The queen of spades has a rank of 10.

(9) *Flat Bet*	A bet of the same amount each time.
(10) *Hole Card*	The dealer's unexposed card.
(11) *Break* (bust)	Exceed 21 points. If a player breaks, he immediately turns over his cards, and the dealer takes his bet. If the dealer breaks, he immediately pays all of the players who did not bust previously.
(12) *Stiff*	Any hand between 12 and 16, inclusive, where the player or dealer has a chance of breaking.
(13) *Push*	A tie between a player and the dealer; no money changes hands.
(14) *Insurance*	A bet allowed when the dealer shows an ace. The player is allowed to bet half his original bet that the dealer has a 10 underneath, and thus a blackjack. If the dealer does have a blackjack, the insurance bet is paid at two to one. The player loses his original bet unless he has a blackjack, in which case his original bet is pushed. If the dealer does not have a blackjack, the insurance bet is lost, and the play continues.
(15) *Surrender*	A decision made by a player to

throw in his first two cards and surrender half his bet. In Nevada this decision is made after it is ascertained that the dealer does not have blackjack. If the player can surrender before the dealer turns his hole card, it is called *early surrender.* Surrender is not permitted in most casinos.

(16) *Split*
A situation in which the player has two like cards (a pair; e.g., 6, 6). He may play the cards as two separate hands, making another bet exactly equal to the amount of his original bet.

(17) *Double Down* (Double)
The doubling of a bet on the first two cards; in this case, the player gets only one more card. Doubling down is advantageous if the player's hand totals 10 or 11, for example, because a 10 would give him a 20 or 21.

(18) *Stand* (Stick)
The player's decision not to take any additional cards.

(19) *System* (Strategy)
The method of play. The basic strategy is an optimized method that involves precise rules for taking insurance, surrendering, splitting, doubling down, hitting,

or sticking. Other systems or strategies involve card-counting for determining favorable player situations, in which case the bet size is increased and the basic strategy is varied.

(20) *Counter*   A player who counts cards.

(21) *Point Count*   The evaluation of odds via a tally of assigned points. A number is assigned to each card according to the value of that card toward making up a winning hand for the player. For example, each 2, 3, 4, 5 or 6 counts as +1; each 7, 8, or 9 counts as 0; each 10, J, Q, K or ace counts as −1. The point count is computed at the end of each hand by adding the counts for each card played in that hand to the point count at the end of the previous hand. For example, if 6, 4, 10, ace, 8, and 3 are dealt off the top of a fresh deck, the point count is +1. This is computed as follows:

Card	Count
6	+1
4	+1
10	−1
A	−1
8	0
3	+1
	+1

(22) *Rank Count*

The number of a particular rank that has been played and counted. Refers to those systems where a particular rank, such as 10s, aces, or 5s, are counted.

(23) *Running Count*

Point count updated as each card is played or dealt by the dealer, rather than at the end of the hand.

(24) *True Count*

Running count adjusted to reflect the number of decks or cards remaining to be played. Also called *count per deck.*

(25) *Player's Advantage* (odds, expectation)

The percent of all money wagered that a player can expect to win in the long run: This number is computed by statistical methods and depends on the particular system the player employs. If a player enjoys a 2 percent advantage, he will win, in the long run, 2 percent of the total amount of money bet. If a player has a 0 percent expectation, he will break even over a period of time. If his expectation is −10 percent, he will eventually lose ten cents out of each dollar bet.

PART I
Background Information

1

The Theory of Winning Blackjack

The theory of winning blackjack involves card counting. The player's probability of winning is dependent upon those cards remaining to be played. Therefore, if the player keeps track of the cards as they are played, he will know what his chances are of winning the next hand. If his chances are better than even, he will raise his bet. If the odds are less than even, he will make a minimum bet. In simpler counting systems, the player does not count all the cards, but only those that most directly affect his probability of winning. These are 10s, aces, and 5s. It has been proven that the odds favor the player when the deck is rich in 10s and aces and short in 5s. In more sophisticated strategies, other cards are also counted.

It is obvious why the deck favors the player when it is rich in 10s and aces: The player will be dealt more blackjacks and more standing hands (19 or 20). The dealer will also receive an equal share of these better hands, but the dealer does not get paid three to two on a blackjack; the dealer cannot double down on a 9, 10, or 11, with a better chance of receiving a 10; the dealer cannot split a pair when the odds are in his favor; the dealer must always hit stiffs (12 to 16) with a better chance of busting.

A surplus of 5s increases the dealer's probability of winning because a 5 will turn any stiff (12 to 16) into a standing hand (17 to 21). Therefore, the fewer 5s there are in the deck, the less the dealer's chance of winning.

The blackjack systems reviewed in this book are all concerned with three vital elements in applying this winning blackjack theory:

• playing the hand;

• counting the cards;

• making the correct-sized bet.

The occasional gambler will learn that there are countless ways that these three elements can be performed and then combined to arrive at a winning strategy. The systems reviewed and analyzed in this book are divided into eight types, representing succeedingly more difficult levels of play:

Type 1:	Progressive Betting Strategies	Type 5:	Level 1 Point-Count Systems

Type 2:	Basic Playing Strategies	Type 6:	Level 2 Point-Count Systems
Type 3:	Rank-Count Systems	Type 7:	Levels 3 and 4 Point-Count Systems
Type 4:	Ten-Count Systems	Type 8:	Ultimate Systems

As the occasional gambler advances from basic play to the more difficult levels of play, his chances of winning and related profit increase, but his level of concentration must also increase. The basic player should understand that successful application of the advanced blackjack systems is dependent upon

• a commitment to learn the system and to invest many hours in practice;

• an ability (which can be learned) to concentrate on card counting while maintaining a casual air;

• the development of the proper attitudes for casino play and money management.

Many of the books reviewed here discuss these success factors at length. Those readers who do not wish to make this commitment should learn the simplified basic strategy and the High-Count System described in Part II of this book.

Players also could be divided into five types, again representing succeedingly more difficult levels of play:

Type	Count System	Playing Strategy	Betting System
Occasional	None	Approximate Basic	Progressive or Hunch
Basic	Simplified Rank-Count	Simplified Basic	Count Betting
Intermediate	Level 1 Point-Count	Basic Strategy	Running-Count
Advanced	Advanced Point-Count	Basic Strategy	True-Count
Professional	Advanced Point-Count	Variations to Basic	True-Count

2

A Brief Review of the Research and Development of Blackjack Systems

I have been a gambler most of my life. I made my first bet in 1946 when I was twelve years old, betting on the St. Louis Cardinals to win the National League pennant and the World Series. I won both bets. In 1956, after graduating from college in Salem, Oregon, I accepted a job in Southern California as a computer programmer trainee in the aerospace industry. Working in Los Angeles afforded me the opportunity to visit Las Vegas about once a month. After two years of consistent losses playing roulette and craps, I discovered the game of blackjack. My background in mathematics and computers motivated me to become a student of the game and to begin investigating scientific methods for beating the game.

I discovered the first scientific study of the game, a book by Baldwin, Cantey, McDermott, and Maisel called *Playing Blackjack to Win*. This book contained the first basic playing strategy and reduced the casino edge from about 6 percent to about 0.25 percent. The strategy was the result of thousands of hours of manual blackjack play by the authors. Applying this basic playing strategy proved very successful and resulted in a series of eighteen successful trips to the Las Vegas casinos. The longest trip was one week in duration to search out the most favorable blackjack playing rules in Nevada. I found that the most favorable rules were in Las Vegas. Until Early Surrender was suspended, the best game was found in the Atlantic City casinos.

The publication of Edward Thorp's *Beat the Dealer* in 1962 revolutionized the game of blackjack. Resulting from extensive computer studies, the book presented the first workable strategy for card counting and varying bet size as the probability of winning fluctuated with the play of the cards. Thorp successfully applied his card-counting strategies in Nevada and the Caribbean.

Thorp's successes inspired many other mathematical and computer scientists to become students of the game, myself among them. I had moved to the Washington, D.C., area in 1961, and had come into contact with Ed Cantey as part of a large army wargaming project. Cantey encouraged Tony Colombo (an expert in probability theory and computer-simulation models) and me to develop a computer simulation of the game of blackjack.

The purpose of this model, to my knowledge the first of its kind, was to evaluate the playing, counting, and betting systems available at that time.

In 1964, the Fall Joint Computer Conference was held in Las Vegas. Tony Colombo and I presented our findings at a session entitled "The Use of Computers in Games of Chance." Chaired by Dr. Thorp, the session was packed with blackjack enthusiasts and would-be card counters. The most popular speaker at the session was Harvey Dubner, who presented his "Hi-Lo" strategy, a simpler and, he claimed, more effective approach than Dr. Thorp's. The presence of Julian Braun, an expert computer scientist with IBM, was also felt during this session. Dr. Braun's computer models and computerized probability calculations have been the basis for all the important blackjack strategy developments in use today.

Two very important effects stemmed from this session. The first involved the casinos; the second involved the subsequent development and application of advanced blackjack strategies. After all the years of having it their own way, the casinos learned that they could be beaten. They panicked! They changed the rules of the game to increase the casino edge and introduced countermeasures, such as shuffling up to reduce the player's advantage. The popularity of the game immediately declined as the average gambler, who was not inclined to learn or apply card-counting methods, stopped playing. The casinos, seeing their profits fall off, reinstated most of the old rules and accepted the fact that a relatively small number of card counters was acceptable if the average player would still keep losing his money. This is still the case today, although the casinos are wary of card counters and bar them from play if they are detected in operation (as I found out the hard way). Many of the systems and books reviewed in Chapter 14 describe how the card counter can disguise his play to avoid detection.

The second outgrowth of the Computer Conference session has also maintained its viability. As the use of existing strategies increased, researchers developed refinements to these strategies and created advanced systems of play. Millions of hands of computerized blackjack have been played during the past fifteen years. Thousands of dollars have been made both selling and using the resulting blackjack strategies. For example, one group of players, working as a team, made over a million dollars by using elaborate hand signals to call in a big bettor when the deck became favorable.

Much of the work in recent years has focused on the avoidance of detection as a card counter. Elaborate but workable ploys have been developed for fooling the dealers and the pit bosses into thinking that the counter is just another average gambler.

I have not been active in developing any of these advanced strategies, but I have been active in using many of them. I have played and won consistently not only in Nevada but also in the Bahamas, San Juan, Europe, and England.

It is important that the reader not jump to the conclusion that blackjack can be used to make easy money. Therefore, prior to reviewing, analyzing, and recommending those systems and strategies that are most effective, I will discuss the barriers to overcome before big profits can be realized.

3

Barriers to Overcome Before Big Profits Can Be Realized

Imagine sitting in a casino at a blackjack table facing a stack of chips. Slot machines are whirring. People are talking. Smoke is drifting in the air. Cocktail waitresses are passing every few minutes pressing drinks. A band is playing in the background. The omnipotent pit boss paces among the tables, watching, looking for unusual bets, searching for the enemy—the counter. . . . As the game progresses, the player is confronted with a never-ending stream of decisions: how much to bet; how many hands to play, how to play the hand; how to maintain the count of the cards. He must decide if the dealer is going to shuffle; if he makes a big bet, and the dealer shuffles, he may be exposed as a counter if he drags his bet back. *Total, absolute concentration is required to make constant decisions and perform precision play.* While doing all of this the player must avoid detection as a counter by exuding the casual, fun-loving attitude of the average losing gambler. Also to avoid detection, he must not play longer than forty-five to sixty minutes in any one casino during a twenty-four to forty-eight hour period. So he is constantly on the move, from casino to casino, during his weekends or vacation.

According to one system seller, these are the rewards of blackjack:

> Everything that money can buy will now be yours
> Independence and security
> A house free and clear of debt
> A life of travel and pleasures
> Financing for your creative ideas
> A college education for your children

The sales literature goes on to say:

> You'll get a permanent Money-Making Machine—a bonafide, accredited system GUARANTEED to give you all the skills necessary to be a specialist in one of the highest-paying fields. You'll use these skills to give yourself an outrageous income of up to $500 a DAY . . . ANY DAY or EVERY DAY . . . anytime you want it!

Let's look at the reasons it is difficult to make "up to $500 a day any day or every day . . ." I am not saying that big money cannot be made playing blackjack; it can. I am contending that it is difficult to make big money or a living playing the game. Here's why!

The casinos are very conscious of card counters. One of the pit bosses' primary duties is to look for them. When a card counter is spotted, the dealer is instructed to shuffle up and the casino puts on the heat; the pit boss walks over and watches the counter to let him know that he is under observation. The counter can disguise his play by making flat bets, but his presence has been noted. If he stays and continues making large bets when the deck is favorable, or if he leaves but returns too soon, he may be barred from that casino. Moving to another area of the casino with a different pit boss is of little use; the word spreads fast. In Atlantic City shuffling up is not permitted, but all the other forms of "heat" can be expected by the player who does not have a good act.

The following are some examples of casino counter-measures from my own experience. I walked into a downtown Las Vegas casino at about eleven one evening. I found a table with only one player (the fewer the players, the greater the number of hands, the higher the profits). I began betting between $25 and $100 (a one-to-four betting scale), depending on my probability of winning. The pit boss watched me increase my bet from $25 to $100 and became extremely nervous. I was playing nonchalantly and talking to the dealer but he was not fooled. I won a quick $800. By then he was literally breathing down my neck. I made flat bets for a while; this didn't fool him. Finally, a very favorable deck occurred that I just couldn't pass up. I bet $100. The dealer shuffled to spoil the rich deck and my favorable winning expectation. Thirty minutes after walking in, I had been detected. I said good night and left.

Another story will illustrate the difficulty of beating the casinos consistently. I was playing in another downtown Las Vegas casino that has very good blackjack rules, e.g., the casino allowed doubling down after splitting a pair. I varied my sessions to about two every three days and played on different shifts so I would not be seen by the same dealers and pit bosses more than once every six days. The first few sessions I was playing a betting scale of $25 to $75. I won a little and didn't attract much attention. I found a friendly dealer—a gal who dealt a few extra hands after the required shuffle point (halfway through the deck) when I had a large bet out. I increased my spread to $25 to $100 and began playing two hands when the deck was favorable. I began to attract the attention of the pit bosses. The dealer was changed halfway through her normal forty-five-minute work cycle. I played a few more hands, watched her get reprimanded by the pit boss, and left about $800 ahead. I stayed away for two days and then returned on a different shift. I noticed some attention from the pit bosses, but not enough to alarm me. I resumed my two-sessions-per-three-days cycle. After about a week, when I was about $1,500 ahead in this casino, a distinguished, well-dressed man walked up to me, presented his card, and introduced himself. He was the casino manager. He complimented me on my "expert" play and told me I made very few mistakes. I mumbled something about being lucky and we chatted a few more minutes. In a very nice way, he asked me not to play there anymore. I got the message.

Besides the casino countermeasures, there are other barriers to overcome before big profits can be realized. Even the simplest of the card-counting systems is difficult to apply in a casino environment. It is easy to make mistakes while counting the cards, anticipating the dealer's shuffle, and settling on a bet size—all within a few seconds. Then, during the play of the hand, the playing strategy may be varied depending upon the composition of the deck. Expert players who have practiced and played under casino conditions for hundreds of hours can do this mental juggling act while holding conversations with the dealer and pit boss. Each novice and intermediate must decide whether or not to make the commitment to become an expert player.

I have played blackjack for twenty years and have spent numerous days in Atlantic City as well as many weekends and vacations in Las Vegas playing blackjack. Yet I still make occasional mistakes in counting, betting, and playing the hand. One hand stands out in my mind. I was playing at the Dunes with a $150 bet and was dealt two aces against the dealer's ace with a true count of −5. Everyone knows you always split aces. Right? Wrong! I split them, drew a small card on each, and lost to the dealer's 20. Against an ace I should have hit and risked losing just $150 instead of $300. Playing precision, perfect blackjack demands a commitment few blackjack players are willing to make because of other priorities. However, less-than-perfect blackjack can still be profitable, as discussed in Parts II and III of this book.

Another element of a successful winning strategy concerns the number of players at the table. The success of many systems is contingent upon there being a maximum of two or three players at a table. This increases the hands played per unit of time and therefore the number of favorable deck situations per unit of time. All this is true, but there are problems in executing this element of a winning strategy. One is the available table space. Even though the Nevada and Atlantic City casinos are expanding, the number of blackjack players is expanding faster. It is difficult to find a table with only two other players, let alone head-to-head play at the two-, five-, and ten-dollar table. Some players are afraid to play head-to-head against the dealer. Countless times when I have found a dealer all to myself, other players have entered the game seconds after I sat down. I was acting as a shill for the house.

The books and system sellers advise playing in the off hours, e.g., 5:00 A.M. to 10:00 A.M. However, many casinos do not keep all their tables open during these off hours. These so-called off hours are usually the most difficult times to play because there are so few available tables.

Another stumbling block to the get-rich-quick scheme is the emotional highs and lows that come from winning and losing. With a bankroll of $500 it is possible to lose $200 or even $300 before starting to win. One of the most difficult problems is maintaining scrupulous attention and playing consistently during the inevitable losing cycles. Conversely, the invincible feeling that follows a winning cycle often leads to careless play. In either situation, carelessness means losses. Remember that the player's advantage averages around 1.0 to 1.5 percent. One mistake every one hundred hands may cost him that edge.

A related problem is the classic problem of "gambler's ruin." Every blackjack book ever written has a section on gambler's ruin. In layman's terms, gambler's ruin means overbetting and, ultimately, going broke. There is a simple formula to follow to avoid gambler's ruin. My rule of thumb is to never make a bet of more than 2 percent of my bankroll. Therefore, when I played a scale of $5 to $20, I carried a $1,000 bankroll. Gambler's ruin is a primary reason every weekend-system player is not taking big money out of the casinos; he goes for the weekend with a few hundred dollars to have a good time. He bets more than he should in proportion to his total bankroll. He goes broke and goes home.

A player should not approach the blackjack table without a game plan. A player should have a stop loss, based on his bankroll, for each session as well as each day if he is on vacation. In addition, most players would be more comfortable with a win stop. This should equal the stop loss. After winning this amount the player should lock up 80 percent of his winnings if he wishes to continue to play.

Finally, the monotony and routine of playing the game for long periods of time work against the player out for big money. Most people are not prepared to sit at a blackjack table for many hours a day for weeks on end. By now, I hope that the reader is in agreement with my caveats about the difficulties in playing full time and making a living from the game. For those of you who are not convinced, I offer one final argument. Of the thousands of system players who play the casinos, how many make their living from the game? Only a few hundred.

Those readers who wish to become part of this select group, together with the readers who would like to supplement their income by playing part time, should study Part III of this book and follow the step-by-step approach recommended there. Readers who gamble occasionally and want at least a better-than-even break against the casino need read no further than Part II.

4

Introduction to Blackjack System Reviews

Chapters 7, 8, 9, and 10 in Part II and Chapters 11 and 12 in Part III contain reviews and analyses of nearly a hundred blackjack systems and strategies. These systems and strategies can be classified into the following types:

Type 1: Progressive Betting Strategies

Type 2: Basic Playing Strategies

Type 3: Rank-Count Systems

Type 4: Ten-Count Systems

Type 5: Level 1 Point-Count Systems

Type 6: Level 2 Point-Count Systems

Type 7: Levels 3 and 4 Point-Count Systems

Type 8: Ultimate Systems

Space limitations prevent a discussion of every blackjack system reviewed. However, all systems are listed and classified in the Appendix. Systems that the reader should avoid as well as the approved strategies are discussed in each chapter.

Reading these six chapters should answer the following questions for the reader:

- What system should I learn that can be expanded to the highest level I might reach in blackjack?

- What systems should I avoid?

- What is the optimum basic playing strategy for one deck? Two decks? Multi-decks?

- Which counting system is the simplest to learn while yielding an acceptable profit?

- What is the most effective advanced blackjack strategy on the market today?

- Should I purchase an advanced blackjack strategy for a hundred dollars? Two hundred dollars?

- What systems, books and other sources of information should I acquire, and how much should it cost to acquire this information?

The Type 3 through Type 8 systems are all concerned with counting cards. The information that a player derives by counting cards is used by him to make two decisions:

- his bet for the next hand, and

• modifications to the basic strategy for the play of the next hand.

Exactly how these decisions are made will be discussed in Chapters 12 and 14. The reader will come out of these six chapters with at least one unanswered question, which will also be taken up in Chapter 14: What is the most effective betting strategy that will yield an acceptable profit but still disguise my play as a card counter?

A major source of review and evaluation of blackjack systems described in these six chapters is *Systems & Methods*, a periodical dedicated to reviewing and evaluating systems and strategies for many gambling games. John Luckman, the publisher, states:

> The art of the criticism process consists of composing, out of experience, judgment, and critical evaluation, something that has instructional value. *Systems & Methods* has brought together a team of experienced evaluators with recognized credentials in their particular fields. We know that everyone will not necessarily agree or disagree with their views; however, their goal is to express their responses with fairness, and look for imagination, quality, and meritorious value in the evoked work.

Systems & Methods originally covered all forms of gambling. In 1977 the publisher separated the coverage of all casino and sports betting and started a new magazine, *Casino & Sports*.

PART II

A Winning Strategy for the Occasional Player

5

A Description of the Basic Playing Strategy

A DISCUSSION OF THE BASIC STRATEGY

It is possible to enjoy a profitable game of blackjack without counting cards by learning and applying the basic playing strategy. Playing a single-deck game with Las Vegas Strip blackjack rules, the player enjoys an advantage of about 0.1 percent, or essentially an even game. The six-deck game in Atlantic City without Early Surrender yields about −0.4 percent; with Surrender, about +0.2 percent—either still essentially an even game. As mentioned earlier, basic strategy has resulted from computer studies totalling millions of hands of simulated blackjack. Julian Braun, for example, played seven million computerized hands to determine the optimum playing strategy for two 4s when the dealer shows a 3, 4, 5, or 6.

I cannot say too often that the basic playing strategy is a must for both casual and serious blackjack players. This is the strategy that the player must use to make the decisions on the play of each hand. These decisions, in the order in which they are made, are insurance (if dealer shows an ace), surrender, split, double down, hit, stand. The basic playing strategy that was devised by Baldwin, Cantey, et al., revised by Thorp, and further revised and developed over the years by Braun is described in this chapter. Currently the most accurate basic playing strategy is the one developed and refined by Braun. However, the reader is cautioned that there are many inaccurate and simplified versions of the basic playing strategy. Also, the literature is replete with many versions of the basic playing strategy that have been made obsolete by recent computer studies. None of these inaccurate, simplified, or obsolete strategies should be learned. All those I could identify by press time are listed in this chapter.

The true basic playing strategies for single-deck, double-deck, and multi-deck play are described in this chapter. Also included are the basic strategies for making insurance and surrender decisions. I have recommended those books and publications where the basic strategy is described in some detail and where learning tools can be found. (These recommendations are repeated in Chapter 18.)

THE SINGLE-DECK STRATEGY

The single-deck strategy is shown in Exhibit 1. This is the most up-to-date basic strategy available in published form. Lawrence Revere's *Playing Blackjack as a Business* provides a good description of the basic strategy and learning aids that amplify Exhibit 1.

Exhibit 1:
Basic Strategy for Las Vegas Single-Deck

Your Hand	Rules for Dealer's Up Cards
8	Double on 5 or 6. Otherwise hit.
9	Double on 2 to 6. Otherwise hit.
10	Double on 2 to 9. Otherwise hit.
11	Always double.
12	Stand on 4 to 6. Otherwise hit.
13 to 16	Stand on 2 to 6. Otherwise hit.
17 to 21	Always stand.
A,2 to A,5	Double on 4 to 6. Otherwise hit.
A,6	Double on 2 to 6. Otherwise hit.
A,7	Double on 3 to 6. Stand on 2, 7, 8, or A. Hit on 9 or 10.
A,8	Double on 6. Otherwise stand.
A,9	Always stand.

Your Hand	Rules for Dealer's Up Cards
A,A	Always split.
2,2	Split on 3 to 7. Otherwise hit.
3,3	Split on 4 to 7. Otherwise hit.
4,4	Treat as 8 above.
5,5	Treat as 10 above.
6,6	Split on 2 to 6. Otherwise hit.
7,7	Split on 2 to 7. Stand on 10. Otherwise hit.
8,8	Always split.
9,9	Split on 2 to 9 except 7. Stand on 7, 10, or A.
10,10	Always stand.

If the casino allows doubling down after splitting pairs (e.g., the El Cortez), you would add the following pair-split rules to those above:

> Split 2,2 on dealer's 2
> Split 3,3 on dealer's 2 and 3
> Split 4,4 on dealer's 4, 5, or 6
> Split 6,6 on dealer's 7
> Split 7,7 on dealer's 8

If the casino allows surrendering, you would modify the above rules and surrender the following hands:

1. Against a dealer's ace you would surrender:

> 10,6

2. Against a dealer's 10 or face card you would surrender:

> 9,6; 9,7; 10,5; 10,6; 7,7

Exhibit 1A:
BASIC STRATEGY FOR RENO/TAHOE SINGLE-DECK

Your Hand	Rules for Dealer's Up Cards
8 or 9	Always hit.
10	Double on 2 to 9. Otherwise hit.
11	Always double.
12	Stand on 4 to 6. Otherwise hit.
13 to 16	Stand on 2 to 6. Otherwise hit.
17 to 21	Always stand.
A,2 thru A,6	Always hit.
A,7	Stand on 2 to 8. Otherwise hit.
A,8 or A,9	Always stand.
A,A	Always split.
2,2	Split on 3 to 7. Otherwise hit.
3,3	Split on 4 to 7. Otherwise hit.
4,4	Always hit.
5,5	Treat as 10 above.
6,6	Split on 2 to 6. Otherwise hit.
7,7	Split on 2 to 7. Stand on 10. Otherwise hit.
8,8	Always split.
9,9	Split on 2 to 9 except 7. Stand on 7, 10, or A.
10,10	Always stand.

- Double down permitted only on 10 or 11.

- Split and resplit any pair.

- No surrender.

- No double down after splitting pairs.

- Dealer hits soft 17.

To better understand Exhibit 1, the reader should take out a deck of cards and deal himself a few hands of blackjack. Try following the rules in Exhibit 1. The strategy may appear formidable and difficult to memorize. A simplified version of the basic strategy, given in Chapter 9, streamlines the strategy to a few simple rules, which provide the reader with 95 percent of the contents of Exhibit 1.

THE NEVADA MULTI-DECK STRATEGIES

The Nevada multi-deck strategies are presented in Exhibit 2. They were derived by Julian Braun and were presented in *How to Play Winning Blackjack*.

THE ATLANTIC CITY MULTI-DECK STRATEGIES

The Atlantic City multi-deck strategies are presented in Exhibit 3. They were also derived by Julian Braun and cover four-, six-, and eight-deck games.

THE INSURANCE DECISION

These comments about the insurance bet apply to all the strategies. The insurance bet is offered to the player when the dealer has an ace showing. The player can bet up to half his original bet that the dealer has a blackjack, with a two-to-one payoff. Mathematically, the insurance bet should never be taken, not even when the player has a blackjack, unless he is counting cards. In the long run, the player will win more by never taking insurance, not even on a blackjack (unless he is counting cards—this will be discussed in Chapters 12 and 14).

THE SURRENDER DECISION

The Surrender strategy for basic play presented in these Exhibits was taken from the computer studies of Julian Braun as published in *How to Play Winning Blackjack*. The Surrender decision can be made on the player's first two cards if the dealer does not show a blackjack. The player is allowed to throw in his hand and surrender half his bet. The player can only surrender after the dealer checks his hand for a blackjack. This is called Late Surrender. Only a few Las Vegas casinos allow this bet.

In Atlantic City Early Surrender was offered. New Jersey law prohibits the dealer from "peeking" at his hole card; thus a player could surrender when the dealer had a blackjack. This rule added about 0.6 percent to the player advantage and resulted in Atlantic City's having the most favorable player advantage in the United States. The rules changes involving the eight-deck game have no effect on basic strategy.

Exhibit 2: Basic Strategy for Nevada Multi-Deck

(with double down after split, single-deck, and double-deck variations)

The following matrix can be used to tailor a basic strategy to any Nevada shoe, single-deck, or double-deck game with the noted rules variations.

Code: [ ]   One-Deck Variations
        (P)   Split if doubling down after splitting allowed—takes precedence over doubling
              on 4,4 versus 5 and 6
        *   Split if DDAS and one-deck

Your Hand	Dealer's Up Card									
	2	3	4	5	6	7	8	9	10	A
5,3	H	H	H	H [D]	H [D]	H	H	H	H	H
6,2	H	H	H	H	H	H	H	H	H	H
9	H [D]	D	D	D	D	D	D	D	H	H
10	D	D	D	D	D	D	D	D	H	H
11	D	D	D	D	D	D	D	D	D	H [D]

Hand										
10,2	H	H	H	H	H	H	H	H	H	H
Other 12s	H	H	S	S	S	H	H	H	H	H
13	S	S	S	S	S	H	H	H	H	H
14	S	S	S	S	S	H	H	H	H	H
15	S	S	S	S	S	H	H	H	H	H
16	S	S	S	S	S	H	H	H	S[H]	S[H]
17 to 21	S	S	S	S	S	S	S	S	S	S
A,2	H	H	H[D]	D	D	H	H	H	H	H
A,3	H	H	H[D]	D	D	H	H	H	H	H
A,4	H	H	D	D	D	H	H	H	H	H
A,5	H	H	D	D	D	H	H	H	H	H
A,6	H[D]	D	D	D	D	H	H	H	H	H
A,7	S	S	S[D]	S[D]	S[D]	S	S	H	H	H[S]
A,8	S	S	S	S	S[D]	S	S	S	S	S
A,9	S	S	S	S	S	S	S	S	S	S
A,A	P	P	P	P	P	P	P	P	P	P[P]

Pair	2	3	4	5	6	7	8	9	10	A
2,2	H(P)	H(P)	P	P	P	P	H	H	H	H
3,3	H(P)	H(P)	P	P	P	P	H	H	H	H
4,4	H	H	H*	H(P) [D]	H(P) [D]	H	H	H	H	H
5,5	D	D	D	D	D	D	D	D	H	H
6,6	H(P) [P]	P	P	P	P	H*	H	H	H	H
7,7	P	P	P	P	P	P	H*	H	H [S]	H
8,8	P	P	P	P	P	P	P	P	P	P
9,9	P	P	P	P	P	S	P	P	S	S
10,10	S	S	S	S	S	S	S	S	S	S

NOTE: If you are playing a two-deck game, the above four-deck strategy should be used with two exceptions:

9—Double on 2-6; otherwise, hit.   11—If 9-2 or 8-3, hit on A. Otherwise, double.

If you are playing a four-deck game, you should use the following surrender strategy.

10,6 vs. a dealer's 9, 10 or A   10,5 vs. a dealer's 10

9,7 vs. a dealer's 9, 10 or A   9,6 vs. a dealer's 10

Exhibit 3:
Basic Strategy for Atlantic City Multi-Deck

Four-, Six-, or Eight-Deck

Your Hand	Rules for Dealer's Up Cards
5 to 8	Always hit.
9	Double on 3 to 6. Otherwise hit.
10	Double on 2 to 9. Hit on 10, A.
11	Double on 2 to 10. Hit on A.
12	Stand on 4 to 6. Otherwise hit.
13	Stand on 2 to 6. Otherwise hit.
14	Stand on 2 to 6. Otherwise hit.
15	Stand on 2 to 6. Otherwise hit.
16	Stand on 2 to 6. Otherwise hit.
17	Always stand.
18 to 21	Always stand.
A,2	Double on 5,6. Otherwise hit.
A,3	Double on 5,6. Otherwise hit.
A,4	Double on 4 to 6. Otherwise hit.
A,5	Double on 4 to 6. Otherwise hit.
A,6	Double on 3 to 6. Otherwise hit.
A,7	Double on 3 to 6. Stand on 2, 7, or 8. Hit on 9, 10, or A.
A,8 to A,10	Always stand.
A,A	Always split.

Your Hand	Rules for Dealer's Up Cards
2,2	Split on 2 to 7. Otherwise hit.
3,3	Split on 2 to 7. Otherwise hit.
4,4	Split on 5,6. Otherwise hit.
5,5	Never split. Treat as 10 above.
6,6	Split on 2 to 6. Otherwise hit.
7,7	Split on 2 to 7. Otherwise hit.
8,8	Always split.
9,9	Split on 2 to 6, 8 or 9. Stand on 7, 10, or A.
10,10	Always stand.

Exhibit 3A:
Basic Strategy for Atlantic City Multi-Deck with Early Surrender

Your Hand	Rules for Dealer's Up Cards
5	Surrender on Ace. Otherwise hit.
6	Surrender on Ace. Otherwise hit.
7	Surrender on Ace. Otherwise hit.
8	Always hit.
9	Double on 3 to 6. Otherwise hit.
10	Double on 2 to 9. Hit on 10 or A.
11	Double on 2 to 10. Hit on A.

12	Stand on 4 to 6. Surrender on A. Otherwise hit.
13	Stand on 2 to 6. Surrender on A. Otherwise hit.
14	Stand on 2 to 6. Surrender on 10 or A. Otherwise hit.
15	Stand on 2 to 6. Surrender on 10 or A. Otherwise hit.
16	Stand on 2 to 6. Surrender on 10 or A. Surrender (10,6 or 9,7)* on 9. Otherwise hit.
17	Surrender on A. Otherwise stand.
18 to 21	Always stand.
A,2	Double on 5 or 6. Otherwise hit.
A,3	Double on 5 or 6. Otherwise hit.
A,4	Double on 4 to 6. Otherwise hit.
A,5	Double on 4 to 6. Otherwise hit.
A,6	Double on 3 to 6. Otherwise hit.
A,7	Double on 3 to 6. Stand on 2, 7, or 8. Hit on 9, 10, or A.
A,8 to A,10	Always stand.
A,A	Always split.
2,2	Split on 2 to 7. Otherwise hit.

*You do not surrender 8,8 on a 9 up-card; only a 10,6 or 9,7.

Your Hand	Rules for Dealer's Up Cards
3,3	Split on 2 to 7. Surrender on A. Otherwise hit.
4,4	Split on 5 or 6. Otherwise hit.
5,5	Never split. Treat as 10 above.
6,6	Split on 2 to 6. Surrender on A. Otherwise hit.
7,7	Split on 2 to 7. Surrender on 10 or A. Otherwise hit.
8,8	Surrender on 10 or A. Otherwise split.
9,9	Split on 2 to 6, 8 or 9. Stand on 7, 10, or A.
10,10	Always stand.

INACCURATE OR OBSOLETE BASIC PLAYING STRATEGIES

The basic playing strategies presented in the previous section are up-to-date and reflect the most recent computer studies. Many strategies, including Dr. Thorp's as published in *Beat the Dealer*, have been superseded by the more recent computer studies of Julian Braun and others. The following books, otherwise containing excellent background material, have inaccurate or obsolete basic strategies:

An Expert's Guide to Winning at 21	Archer, J.
Beat the Dealer	Thorp, E. O.
Scientific Blackjack and Complete Casino Guide	Collver, D. I.
The Casino Gamblers' Guide	Wilson, A. N.
The Theory of Gambling and Statistical Logic	Epstein, R. A.
Winning at Casino Gaming	Staff of Rouge et Noir
21 Counting Methods to Beat 21	Ita, K.

PROGRESSIVE BETTING SYSTEMS (TYPE 1)

There are any number of strategies touted as blackjack systems that are merely progressive betting systems, sometimes combined with a basic strategy. Unless you count cards, blackjack becomes just another casino game of independent trials and no betting method ever has been or ever will be devised that can overcome the negative expectations of these games. The following systems fall in this category and cannot be recommended.

Basic Blackjack Betting	Einstein, C.
Blackjack Profits	McCall, Whit
Blackjack (21) Solitaire	Bollinger, J.
Crayne System	Crayne, C.
Greatest Blackjack Revolutionary Method	Tarkin, M.

BASIC PLAYING SYSTEMS (TYPE 2)

Also available are a number of so-called blackjack systems that are only an explanation of the rules of the game or a presentation and a method of learning basic strategy. These include booklets, charts, slide rules, and rotating discs. *The Facts of Blackjack* by Walter I. Nolan is available at almost any bookstore that carries casino games books and costs one dollar. This booklet, together with the appropriate basic strategy from this chapter and some practice, is all you need to play a perfect basic strategy game anywhere in the world. Subsequently none of the following systems can be recommended:

Atvada Proven Method of Play	Atvada Associates
Beat the Dealer Blackjack Computer	Technical Research of Florida Inc.
Blackjack Calculator	Roden, C. W.
Blackjack: How to Improve Your Playing Strategy in the Game of 21, When You Are Holding 12-13-14-15-16	Dr. Ace Jack
Blackjack Mate	Blackjack Mate, Florida
Blackjack-O-Matic	Game Theory Consultants
Blackjack Winning Wheel	Artech Products
How to Beat Blackjack Dealers	Atherton, R. and B.
Instant Blackjack Answers Wheel	Practical Products Co.
Magic Wheel of Blackjack	Lane Publishing Co.
Morgan Method	Morgan, T.
New Key to Winning at Blackjack	Major Winnings Co.
The Uston	Uston, K.
Winning Blackjack Simplified	Pine, A.
Winning Gamblers Pocket Computer	Scientific Research Services
Z-System	Bennett, L.

Some of the slide rules and rotating discs, such as *The Uston,* would be valuable to the novice player if he could use them at the table. But in Atlantic City many pit bosses will not even permit the use of basic strategy cards.

6

A Review of Rank-Count Systems (Ace-Five, Type 3; Ten-Count, Type 4)

As the name implies, rank-count systems involve counting certain rank cards, usually aces, 5s, and 10s. They differ from point-count systems in which a value is assigned to each card type (e.g., 10s count as -2, non-10s count as $+1$) and a running count kept as the cards are played.

ACE-FIVE–COUNT SYSTEMS (TYPE 3)

In Thorp's computer and analytic studies, he noticed that the removal of certain cards from the deck has an influence on the player's expectation of winning. He discovered that the card with the largest positive impact is the 5. When all four 5s have been played, the player's advantage using the basic strategy increases from about 0.1 percent to about 3.6 percent. Conversely, when a deck is depleted of aces, the player's advantage decreases to about −2.4 percent. Thorp developed a strategy that involved counting 5s. When the deck is devoid of 5s, the player's bet is increased. He refined this strategy by relating the number of 5s remaining to be played to the number of remaining cards. When the ratio of cards remaining in the deck to 5s remaining is less than thirteen, the player makes a small bet; when greater than thirteen, the player makes a big bet. A similar but converse strategy was developed for the aces. A deck rich in aces favors the player.

In today's casino environment, these systems are virtually obsolete unless played with another counting system, since in most casinos only half a single deck and slightly more of a double deck is dealt before the deck is reshuffled. The one-third cut in the four- and six-deck games is only slightly more favorable. This shuffling limits the number of favorable occurrences. The advent of more powerful blackjack strategies also contributed to the obsolescence of these simple counting systems.

Still, there are two reasons the player should consider learning a simple ace-five–count system:

• Use of the system provides valuable training for the more advanced counting systems.

- The system may function as a side count as a part of a more effective blackjack counting system.

Because of their simplicity there are few other systems in this category to comment upon. Stanley Roberts presents a simple ace count and a five-six count in his book *Winning Blackjack*, and has taught it in his school. Lawrence Revere offered a five-count strategy in *Playing Blackjack As a Business* as a means of training for a more advanced count. Ken Uston also presents the ace-five count in *Million-Dollar Blackjack* but adds, "It's a strategy meant for the recreational player who, we hope, is betting at low levels in the casino."

Ace-Five–Count Systems (Type 3)

Revere Five-Count Strategy	Revere, L.
Roberts Ace Count	Roberts, S.
Roberts Five-Six Count	Roberts, S.
Thorp Five Count	Thorp, E. O.
Uston Ace-Five Count	Uston, K.

TEN-COUNT SYSTEMS (TYPE 4)

Until a few years ago, ten-count systems were the workhorse strategies used by most of the serious blackjack players. Although they were effective and widely used, most serious players generally have progressed to the point-count systems discussed in Part III.

The problem with a ten-count system is that it is difficult to learn, and difficult to use. Two numbers must be remembered: 10s and non-10s. There are sixteen 10s in a deck and thirty-six others. The player can start with a count of 0, 0 and count forward or begin with a 36, 16 count and count backward, Thorp's approach. The ten-count system is more accurate than the simpler point-count systems, since it takes into account the number of cards played. Therefore, the player must choose simplicity and ease of play or accuracy. My recommendation to the reader will follow a brief review of the ten-count systems. Many ten-count systems were reviewed. Most were simplifications of Thorp's original system and not as accurate as the original system.

The Thorp ten-count system involves a starting count of 36 (others) and 16 (10s) for single-deck play. The player counts backward as the cards are played. To determine his advantage, the player computes a ratio of others to 10s. A full deck ratio equals $^{36}/_{16}$ or 2.25. When the ratio is 2.0 or less the player makes a larger bet than his minimum—the lower the ratio, the higher the bet. Thorp's system is not recommended because it involves remembering two numbers (10s, others) and computing one other (the ratio). Thorp's modifications to the basic playing strategy for different values of the ratio (less than or equal to 2.0) are presented in complicated tables and are very difficult to learn. It should be remembered, however, that Thorp's system is the genesis for all simplified and advanced blackjack strategies.

Though Revere claims his ten-count system is simpler to learn than the Thorp ten-count, it is, in my view, much

more difficult to learn. It involves memorizing complicated tables and codes. Tens and others are counted
starting with 0, 0. These two numbers are converted to a
code, which must be looked up in a table to determine the
proper bet size. Revere himself seems to give up on
learning this complicated table by presenting a simplified
chart that leaves out "half of the codes to make it easier to
learn." He then admits to not memorizing this table by
stating that he had the table engraved on a cigarette
lighter. "The lighter would be in front of me at all times
when I played." Revere's codes are also used to modify the
basic playing strategy when the odds favor the player.
Memorizing these modifications is just as difficult as
memorizing the code tables. Revere's system is not recommended.

Roberts' ten-count system involves the learning of
tables, although these tables are not nearly so complicated
as Revere's. The system starts with a count of 0, 0.
Learning the tables eliminates the necessity of calculating
the Thorp ratio. Table values indicate whether the deck is
rich (in 10s), poor, very rich, or very poor. The player bets
accordingly. The tables have an arithmetic logic to them,
and the player can easily compute table values by following a simple formula. There are separate tables for single-
deck, two-deck, and four-deck games. I found that
Roberts' tables were difficult to memorize but that it was
fairly easy to compute their value by using the simple
formula. This computation is comparable to the computation of Thorp's ratio. As Thorp's ratio provides the player
with more accuracy, Thorp's ten-count system is rated
superior to Roberts'. Julian Braun computed the player's

advantage for a one-to-four betting scale as 1.9 percent using Thorp's ten-count, as opposed to 1.5 percent for Roberts'.

It should be noted that since the publication of *Winning Blackjack*, Roberts has developed a simplified version of his system that eliminates the need to learn the tables. However, for the reasons already noted, I cannot recommend any of the ten-count systems listed below.

Ten-Count Systems (Type 4)

Archer System	Archer, J.
Goldberg Computer System	Goldberg, A.
Kalinevitch Ten Count	Kalinevitch, D.
Noir One-Two Count	Noir, J.
Revere Ten Count	Revere, L.
Roberts' Ten Count	Roberts, S.
Sum Plus One	Watson, George III
Thorp Ten Count	Thorp, E. O.

For the player with only a few hours to devote to learning a system that will provide a small edge over the casino, I have developed an ace-ten–count system that is easy to learn, simple to use, and quite effective. The system is actually a simplified version of the high-low system. It is called High-Count and is discussed in the next chapter.

7

A Winning Strategy That Can Be Learned in About Two Hours

The systems described in this chapter will prove extremely useful to the occasional player who does not wish to invest the time to learn every single rule of the basic strategy or to master simple or sophisticated card counting techniques. The systems have been mastered by many players I have taught, including my wife.

SIMPLIFIED BASIC STRATEGY

I realize I am leaving myself open to criticism in presenting my own simplified basic strategy after previously criticizing others. There is one difference, however. In my simplified strategy, the player chooses the degree of error he is willing to live with. The player's error is reduced to just 1 percent after he has learned the fourteen rules of the simplified basic strategy. The interested player can easily eliminate this 1 percent when he is ready, by studying Chapter 7.

The playing strategy described in this chapter is based on a simple premise: Rules should be learned in accordance with the frequency of occurrence of the hands the rule governs. For example, if the player is dealt hands totaling 12 to 16 thirty-seven percent of the time, then he should learn the rule governing these hands before he learns a rule governing hands that occur only 10 percent of the time.

The player should learn the basic strategy rules in Exhibit 4 in the order they are given and should concentrate on the first twelve rules. The simplified basic strategy presented in Exhibit 4 can be played for one-, two-, or multi-deck games. Minor errors occur in the two- and multi-deck games. The player so inclined can correct these errors by modifying the simplified strategy with the contents of Exhibit 2. These errors affect only about 1.7 percent of the hands dealt, so the occasional player may not wish to invest the time.

The player using the simplified basic strategy should not lose more than about 1 percent of his 0.1 percent edge for a one-deck game and about 2 percent of his −0.4 percent expectation for a multi-deck game without surrender.

THE HIGH-COUNT SYSTEM

You have the advantage when the remaining deck(s) is rich in 10s and aces. That's when you should increase your bet.

The High-Count system was developed for the player who does not wish to invest the time required to learn the more complicated strategies. Counting high cards only is much easier than scanning every card to update a point count.

You play this system by counting 10s and aces and watching the discards or discard tray. You must be able to approximate the remaining deck(s) in the game. This is done by estimating the discards and subtracting this number from the total deck(s) in the game; e.g., in a six-deck game, if you estimate one deck is in the discard tray, then there are five decks remaining. In a one-deck game, if you estimate one-quarter of a deck has been played, then three-quarters of a deck remains.

Select and learn the table in Exhibit 5 for the game you will be playing. Bet one unit when the total count of the high cards seen is normal or above. When fewer than normal high cards have been seen, bet according to the table.

This system approximates betting one unit per High-Low true count, and will be slightly off whenever a surplus of 7s, 8s, and 9s has been played.

Exhibit 4:
Simplified Basic Strategy

Rule No.	Surrender
1	In Atlantic City if permitted, surrender 5 to 7 and 12 to 17 against dealer's ace. Surrender 14 to 16 against dealer's 10.

HITTING/STANDING RULES

2	Always stand on 12 to 16 if dealer shows 2 to 6; otherwise hit.
3	Always stand on 17 or above (hard hands). Hit until you get 17 if dealer shows 7 to A.
4	Always hit 17 or less (soft hands), if you can't double down.
5	Always stand on 18 or above (soft hands).

DOUBLE DOWN RULES

6	Double on 11 if dealer shows 2 to 10.
7	Double on 10 if dealer shows 2 to 9.
8	Double on 9 if dealer shows 3 to 6.
9	Double on A,2 to A,7 if dealer shows 4 to 6.

Rule No.	Surrender
	RULES FOR SPLITTING PAIRS
10	Always split aces, 8s.
11	Never split 10s, 5s, or 4s.
12	Split 2s, 3s, 6s, 7s, and 9s when dealer shows 4 to 6.
	REFINEMENTS TO FIRST 12 RULES
13	Hit 12 if dealer shows a 2 or 3.
14	Hit soft 18 when dealer shows 9, 10, or A.

A SIMPLIFIED BETTING METHOD

Your high bet should not exceed 2 percent of your casino bankroll; that is, the total of the money you have set aside to play blackjack. Divide the high bet by the number of units at the high bet to determine your unit bet and table minimum. For example, if your bankroll is $1,500, in a six-deck game your high bet would be $30 (2 percent of $1,500), and your unit bet would be $5 ($30 divided by 6). You should play at a $5 minimum table.

Caution: This system is not as effective as the point-count systems discussed in later chapters. Your long-run advantage with High-Count is about 0.3 percent as compared to about 1.0 to 1.5 percent for the point-count systems.

Exhibit 5: The High-Count System

Eight-Deck Game

Remaining Decks	NORMAL COUNT	ACTUAL COUNT		
		2-Unit Bet	3-Unit Bet	4-Unit Bet
7	20	6		
6	40	28	16	4
5	60	50	40	30
4	80	72	64	56

Six-Deck Game

Remaining Decks	NORMAL COUNT	ACTUAL COUNT		
		2-Unit Bet	4-Unit Bet	6-Unit Bet
5	20	10	0	
4	40	32	24	16
3	60	54	48	42
2	80	76	72	68

Four-Deck Game

Remaining Decks	NORMAL COUNT	ACTUAL COUNT		
		2-Unit Bet	4-Unit Bet	6-Unit Bet
3	20	14	8	2
2	40	36	32	28
1	60	58	56	54

Two-Deck Game

Remaining Decks	NORMAL COUNT	ACTUAL COUNT		
		2-Unit Bet	3-Unit Bet	4-Unit Bet
1½	10	7	5	4
1	20	18	17	16
½	30	29		28

One-Deck Game

Remaining Decks	NORMAL COUNT	ACTUAL COUNT		
		2-Unit Bet	3-Unit Bet	4-Unit Bet
¾	5		3	2
½	10	9		8
¼	15			14

PART III

A Review and Analysis of Intermediate and Advanced Winning Strategies

8

An Analysis of Point-Count Systems

DEFINITION OF POINT-COUNT SYSTEMS

A point-count system involves assigning a plus or minus value to each card rank. As noted in Chapter 4, the first point-count system was developed by Harvey Dubner and was presented at the 1964 Fall Computer Conference. It was called "Hi-Lo" and involved the assignment of a simple plus or minus value to each card. Braun expanded Dubner's system and developed a workable but still simple point-count system, which was published in the second edition of Thorp's book. This initial development led to the development of many other point-count systems.

The characteristics of a Level 1 point-count system are listed below:

- No more than three values are assigned to the various card types (usually +1, 0, and −1).

- The running count is used to vary the bet size at a primary level. The true count is used for precise betting at an advanced level.

- Variations to the basic strategy are available at the advanced level.

- The system usually includes an optional side count of aces at the advanced level.

The basic differences among the Level 1 point-count systems are

    1. the values of the various card ranks
    2. the ease of learning the system
    3. the variations to the basic strategy associated with each system when the odds favor the player
    4. the price.

These four differences plus the player's advantage are used as the evaluation criteria.

LEVEL 1 POINT-COUNT SYSTEMS (TYPE 5)

The following group of Level 1 Point-Count systems all are designed so the intermediate player can start with a simple system using the running count for betting and playing basic strategy. The player may then choose to progress to an advanced level and learn to use the true count for more optimal bet sizing. Finally the player may opt for the professional level, learning to use the true count for precise variations to the basic strategy. With the exception of Ken Uston's Advanced Plus Minus, all these systems provide for a side count of aces for even more exact insurance and playing decisions. All these systems are approved and selected for further evaluation.

Canfield Expert	Canfield, R. A.
DHM Professional	Mitchell, D. H.
High-Low	Braun, J. H., or Wong, S.
Hi Opt I	Humble, L.
Uston Advanced Plus Minus	Uston, K.

The next group of point-count systems were the best available when they were introduced, but they are now considered obsolete or have been replaced with newer systems using the same count values but with more detailed and up-to-date playing strategies.

Collver Scientific Blackjack	Collver, D. I.
Dubner Hi-Lo	Dubner, H.
Einstein Counting System	Einstein, C.
Gordon System	Gordon, E.
Green Fountain Strategy	Ita, K.
Mayer Count System	Mayer, G.
McGhee Plus Minus System	McGhee, W. B.
Revere Plus Minus Strategy	Revere, L.
Revere Advanced Plus Minus	Revere, L.
Rouge et Noir System	Staff of Rouge et Noir
Skovand Single-Column System	Skovand, D.
Thorp Complete Point-Count	Thorp, E. O.
Ultimate Blackjack System	Miliman, M. H.

The final group of point-count systems are classified as having some value. They are not recommended since they contain no method for the developing player to convert to true count for more precise betting or varying the basic strategy.

Aus the Boss Blackjack System	Computerized Systems Institute
Austin's Starter System	Austin
Carter R.P.I.	Sci-Rater
Conklin System	Conklin, J. B.
Mini Blackjack	Circuit, F.

Boyd Play Better Blackjack	Boyd, C.
Roberts One Number Register	Roberts, S.
Wilson Point-Count	Wilson, A. N.

There are at least two noncounting systems being offered that rely on an approximation of a point count. They are based on an observation that certain types of hands tend to use an abnormal amount of high or low cards and therefore possibly create a favorable or unfavorable condition. The systems require being able to recognize these sequences or situations and then raise or lower the bet size.

This type of system is doubly dangerous. First, any such approximation cannot be accurate enough to risk an increased bet, and second, a favorable sequence could occur as easily as not in a negative deck. Increasing the bet in a negative-expectation situation goes against all known winning blackjack theory. In addition, using these approximations to vary basic strategy is in my opinion ridiculous. The two systems to avoid are:

No Need to Count	Dubey, Leon B. Jr.
Situation and Sequence	Grant, Doug

Exhibit 6:
Comparison of Level 1 Point-Count Systems

System	A	2	3	4	5	6	7	8	9	10	Latest Price
Thorp (converted 10 count)	4	4	4	4	4	4	4	4	4	−9	$ 2.45
Dubner, Thorp, Braun	−1	1	1	1	1	1	0	0	0	−1	$12.95
Revere, Rouge et Noir, Wong, Wilson	4	−1	−1	−1	−1	−1	−1	−1	−1	1	$19.95
Collver	0	$\frac{1}{3}$	$\frac{1}{3}$	$\frac{1}{3}$	$\frac{1}{3}$	$\frac{1}{3}$	$\frac{1}{3}$	$\frac{1}{3}$	$\frac{1}{3}$	−$\frac{2}{3}$	$ 1.95
Einstein, Austin, Hi Opt I	0	0	1	1	1	1	0	0	0	−1	$14.95
J. Noir (unbalanced count)	−2	1	1	1	1	1	1	1	1	−2	$11.95
Revere Advanced Plus Minus	0	1	1	1	1	1	0	0	−1	−1	$25.00
Roberts, Goldberg, Archer (unbalanced converted 10 count)	1	1	1	1	1	1	1	1	1	−2	$95.00
Gordon, DHM	0	1	1	1	1	0	0	0	0	−1	$95.00

System											Price
Systems Research	-1	1	1	1	1	1	1	0	-1	-1	$25.00
McGhee	1	1	1	1	1	0	1	-1	-1	-1	$50.00
Scovand	0	1	1	1	1	1	1	1	0	100	$20.00
Ita	-1	1	1	1	1	1	1	0	-1	-1	$ 2.00
Canfield Expert	0	0	1	1	1	1	1	0	-1	-1	$10.00
Uston Advanced Plus Minus	-1	0	1	1	1	1	1	0	0	-1	$14.95

Systems are listed in the order of date published

9

An Analysis of Advanced Blackjack Strategies

Stanford Wong earns his living playing blackjack and plays with impunity in casinos throughout the world. Lawrence Revere made as much as fifty thousand dollars in a single month. Ian Andersen has made his living in Las Vegas for over ten years. Ken Uston led a team of blackjack players that made over a million dollars. All of these blackjack players had one thing in common: They used an advanced blackjack strategy.

What qualifications are necessary to join these select few? A logical mind, the ability to make rapid mental calculations, an excellent memory, a meticulous power of concentration, and lots of self-confidence. Still with me?

Go fix yourself a drink and then find a quiet room where you will not be disturbed. The following paragraphs are complicated.

DISCUSSION OF THE TRUE COUNT

A major characteristic of an advanced blackjack strategy is the use of a true count—the adjustment of the running count for the number of decks remaining.

The true count is computed by dividing the running count by the number of decks or fraction of deck remaining to be played. The reader can visualize the effect of this adjustment by considering the following example. In a point-count system where small cards (2 to 6) count + 1, 7 to 9 count zero, and high cards (aces, 10) count − 1, let us assume the running count is + 5. Very early in a one-deck game the true count would equal + 5 (running count divided by remaining decks or + 5 divided by one). When one-fourth of the deck remains to be played, the true count would equal + 20 (+ 5 divided by one-fourth, or five times four). What is the significance of this variation? In the beginning of the deck it means that five more small cards have been played than high cards. Off the top of a fresh deck, there are twenty small cards, so fifteen are left to be played. But at the end of the deck, the significance is much greater. In the extreme, if only five cards remain to be played, they are all 10s and aces! The deck is much more favorable to the player. This condition is reflected in a higher number when the running count is divided by the number of remaining decks.

If a player intends to use an advanced strategy, he must learn to use the true count. This is not as difficult as it seems. The true count does not have to be computed exactly. You can approximate by estimating the decks or half-decks remaining to be played. If, for example, in a one-deck game, three-fourths of the deck remains to be played, you divide the running count by three-fourths or simply increase the running count by one-third. For this example, if the running count is +3, the true count is +4. If the running count is +4, the true count is +5 (you round off).

Because of the significance of the true count to advanced strategy play, Exhibit 7 is included. This exhibit shows the differences between the running count and true count for the High-Low point-count strategy and for one-, two-, four-, and six-deck play. Before reviewing this exhibit, the reader should understand that the running count usually varies between +6 and −6. However, extremely high values of the running count are used for illustrative purposes. Also for illustrative purposes only, exact values of the true count are shown.

If all this seems too complicated, take heart, for many methods of learning to play intermediate, advanced, and professional blackjack are now available to the beginning player. These methods include blackjack courses either at a school or by mail; see Chapters 17 and 18.

Exhibit 7:
Relationship Between True Count and Running Count

Cards Played	High-Low Running Count	True Count One-Deck	True Count Two-Deck	True Count Four-Deck	True Count Six-Deck	True Count Eight-Deck
10, 5, 6, 6, 8, A, 4, 8	2	2.4	1.1	.5	.3	.3
7, 9, 10, 2, 6, 3, 10, 7, 9	3	4.5	1.8	.8	.5	.4
5, 8, 4, A, 10, 2, 3, 4	6	11.6	3.9	1.7	1.1	.8
5, 3, 4, 7, 9, 10, 2, 6	10	27.4	7.3	3.0	1.9	1.4
10, 8, 9, 3, 7, 2, 5	12	52.0	9.8	3.7	2.3	1.7
10, 10, A, 10, 10, A	6	52.0	5.4	1.9	1.2	.8
10, 10, 10, 10, 10, 10	0	0	0	0	0	0

NOTE: The values on each line are cumulative and assume the cards on all of the previous lines have been played.

Several interesting conclusions can be inferred from Exhibit 7

• The difference between the true count and the running count increases as cards are dealt and played.

• The greater the number of decks, the smaller the variation of the true count from 0; this is one reason multi-deck play is less favorable to the player.

• Bet size variations will be drastic between the running count and true count for one-, two-, four-, six-, and eight-deck play.

The true count is used to vary both the bet size and the basic strategy. The running count could be used to do this, but the true count is much more accurate.

Advanced strategy decision rules are usually based on one of two methods for computing the true count:

$$1. \text{ true count} = \frac{\text{running count}}{\text{remaining deck(s)}}$$

$$2. \text{ true count} = \frac{\text{running count}}{\text{remaining half-deck(s)}}$$

The use of one or the other method is reflected in the basic strategy tables which indicate when the playing decisions (e.g., hit or stand) are made based on the value of the true count. In general, table values for the first method are computed on fifty-two cards remaining to be played. Table values for the second method are computed on twenty-six cards remaining to be played. The recommendations in this book are for systems employing the first method. Both methods are applicable to one-, two-, four-, six-, and eight-deck games.

Exhibit 8 shows how the true count is used to vary the basic strategy. This exhibit is included for illustrative purposes only and may not represent the recommended strategy for hitting or standing for all counting systems.

DIFFERENCES BETWEEN INTERMEDIATE AND ADVANCED LEVEL 1 POINT-COUNT SYSTEMS

Advanced blackjack strategies differ in several ways from intermediate Level 1 point-count systems that use the running count for betting and basic strategy for playing. Many of the advanced strategies attempt to approximate the actual value of each card rank toward the composition of the player's hand. For example, the strategy would establish whether or not a deck rich in 7s is more favorable to the player than a deck rich in 3s. If so, the 7 would receive a value to reflect this difference. Consequently, the card values for these advanced point-count systems are usually more complicated than for Level 1 point-count systems. We shall see, nevertheless, that a Level 1 point-count system can be enhanced so that it can emerge as a complete advanced point-count system.

Another difference is in the variations to the basic playing strategy to take advantage of the true count. For example, basic strategy indicates doubling down on 9 when the dealer shows 2 to 6 (single deck). However, for certain values of the true count, the player would double down on 9 when the dealer shows 2 to 7. Another good example is the insurance decision. The player can add about 0.2 percent to his advantage by using the true count to make the insurance decision. Variations to the basic strategy can be relatively simple for Level 1 point-count systems, and sometimes reflect a narrower point-count range than the higher-level systems. For advanced black-jack systems it is important to learn the strategy variations for various ranges of the true count. For a six-deck game, for example, the player might learn strategy changes for the true count range −1 to +1. Situations for strategy changes outside this range do not occur as often and could be learned in conjunction with an advanced system. The range −2 to +3 might be learned first; then −2 to +7.

Many advanced blackjack strategies involve the use of side counts, usually aces. These side counts can also be kept with Level 1 point-count systems, but may be used differently. In systems that value the ace as 0, a side count is used mainly to increase the player's bet under the proper circumstances. In advanced blackjack strategies, they are also used for precision play. When there is a shortage of aces, for example, the player would not double down on 10 against a dealer's 10 in a favorable deck; otherwise he would do so.

An advanced blackjack system may or may not include the use of a point-count system higher than Level 1. The difference in the levels is the number of values assigned to the various card types. A Level 2 point-count system uses

+2 and −2 in addition to the +1, 0, and −1 used at
Level 1. A Level 3 system adds the digit 3 and the Level 4
adds the digit 4. Needless to say, the higher the system
level, the more difficult it is to learn and the more difficult
it is to use.

Exhibit 8:
Examples of Variations to the Basic Strategy
with the True Count

PLAYER'S HAND				DEALER'S UP CARD						
	2	3	4	5	6	7	8	9	10	A
12	+3	+2	0	−2	−1	H	H	H	H	H
13	−1	−2	−4	−5	−5	H	H	H	H	H
14	−4	−5	−7	−8	−8	H	H	H	H	H
15	−6	−7	−8	S	S	H	H	+8	+4	H
16	−7	S	S	S	S	H	+7	+5	0	+8

H = always hit

S = always stand

Stand if the true count value
equals or is greater
than the table value.

All advanced blackjack systems use the true count for optimal betting and precise strategy variations. In addition, the systems that assign the ace a value of 0 usually require a side count of aces for betting purposes. With systems that do give a value to the ace, the side count is optional and is used primarily for perfect insurance decisions.

As we found at Level 1, the basic differences among the higher level point-count systems include

1. the value of the various card ranks
2. the ease of learning the sysem
3. the variations to the basic strategy associated with each system when the odds favor the player
4. the price.

Again, these four differences plus the player's advantage are used as the evaluation criteria.

LEVEL 2 POINT-COUNT SYSTEMS (TYPE 6)

The following Level 2 point-count systems are complete advanced point-count systems and are approved and selected for further evaluation.

Canfield Master	Canfield, A.
Hi Opt II	Humble, L.
R & T Complete Point Count Strategy	Francis, M.

The next Level 2 point-count systems are not recommended, as the currently available playing strategies are either obsolete or incomplete. The Accu-Count System has the same card values as Hi Opt II but the playing strategy has no numbers for surrender or multi-deck games.

Accu-Count System	Accu-Count Inc.
AWK Count	Witcombe, D.
Reppert Blackjack System	Reppert, J.
Revere Point-Count Strategy	Revere, L.

LEVELS 3 AND 4 POINT-COUNT SYSTEMS (TYPE 7)

These three systems are complete advanced point-count systems and are approved and will be further evaluated.

Revere APC 1973	Revere, L.
Uston APC	Uston, K.
Wong Halves	Wong, S.

The first high-level system ever published is now obsolete and is not recommended. It has been replaced by the Revere APC 1973.

Revere APC 1971	Revere, L.

Exhibit 9:
Comparison of Levels 2, 3, and 4 Point-Count Systems

System	Level	C / A	a / 2	r / 3	d / 4	5	V / 6	a / 7	l / 8	u / 9	e / 10	Latest Price
Reppert	2	-2	1	1	1	2	1	1	0	-1	-1	$100.00
Revere Point Count	2	-2	1	2	2	2	2	1	0	0	-2	$ 9.95
Revere APC 1971	4	-4	2	3	3	4	3	2	0	-1	-3	$200.00
Revere APC 1973	4	0	2	2	3	4	2	1	0	-2	-3	$200.00
Hi Opt II, Accu-Count	2	0	1	1	2	2	1	1	0	0	-2	$200.00
Uston APC	3	0	1	2	2	3	2	2	1	-1	-3	$ 14.95
Wong Halves	3	-1	.5	1	1	1.5	1	.5	0	-.5	-1	$ 19.95
Canfield Master	2	0	1	1	2	2	2	1	0	-1	-2	$250.00
A W K	2	-2	1	1	1	2	1	0	0	0	-1	$ 10.00
R & T	2	0	1	1	2	2	2	0	0	0	-2	$ 10.00

Systems are listed in the order of date published

ULTIMATE SYSTEMS (TYPE 8)

When the man who started it all, Edward O. Thorp, published *Beat the Dealer* in 1962, he included an "Ultimate Strategy." This involved assigning to the various card types values ranging from -9 to $+11$, keeping this count for perfect betting, and simultaneously using the ten-count, which in itself was too difficult for most players, for insurance and strategy variations. I know of no one person who has successfully implemented this combination system.

In 1966 Donald I. Collver described an "Advanced Casing" system in *Scientific Blackjack and Complete Casino Guide*. It amounted to keeping track of aces, 10s, small cards (2 through 5), and medium cards (6 through 9). This system also proved to be too cumbersome for mere mortals.

Edward Gordon devised a counting system using the same card groups; this was published in the *Claremont Economic Papers* in 1973. The strategy was subsequently developed into the DHM systems and was discussed at length in *Gambling Times,* February 1978, under the name of D. Howard Mitchell.

Bert Fristedt and David Heath brought forth still another system using the same card values and groups in 1975. The strategy was published complete in *Winning,* May 1977. Even though the system has been clearly defined, I know of no person who has been able to use it in the casino.

Still another approach to the ultimate system was

presented by Peter Griffin in 1975, called "Multiple Parameters." This strategy, detailed in Griffin's book *The Theory of Blackjack*, requires keeping separate counts of card types not counted in a card-counting system. It was first applied to the Hi-Opt strategies and involved keeping side counts of 2s, 3s, 7s, 8s, and 9s as well as the usual aces. Other than Griffin himself, who tracks everything except 2s, I know of no one with the mental agility to use this system successfully.

David Sklansky suggested the "Key Card Concept" in an article in *Gambling Times*, August 1977. The strategy necessitates keeping track of every card type in the deck and is possible only in a single-deck game. Only a handful of players are capable of doing this in an actual game.

D. Howard Mitchell applied the "Key Card Concept" to his DHM Expert system and called it the DHM Ultimate. He describes this system as "an academic device which is being developed only to find out how close to . . . ultimate performance this . . . system comes." The description, I suggest, covers all ultimate systems.

CHOOSING A BLACKJACK SYSTEM

Selecting a particular system is an important decision for a blackjack player. A system once thoroughly learned is not easily "unlearned" and replaced with another. Ken Uston developed and sells the Uston Advanced Point Count but still personally uses the 1973 Revere Advanced Point Count, even though it is slightly less powerful and is more complicated than his own system.

The student faced with three levels of blackjack play—intermediate, advanced, and professional—cannot know initially what level he will finally attain. For this reason, when a player advances beyond basic strategy and chooses a card-counting system, I suggest that he select one that is usable at the advanced and professional levels and is comparable in efficiency with all other systems available at each level.

In addition to this recommended flexibility, the student must consider the ease of learning the system, its cost in dollars, and its relative betting and playing efficiency.

For the average blackjack student, comparing the efficiencies of the various blackjack systems to find the most favorable advantage can be a bewildering experience. The majority of comparison schedules have been published by system sellers and the data is often slanted to portray their particular system in the best possible light.

In addition, systems counting the ace as 0 and requiring a side count of aces are frequently compared to systems counting the ace as a high card with an optional side count, without indicating the increased efficiencies obtained when the ace side count is used.

Even more confusion is caused by the fact that systems are available with up to 100 percent *betting efficiency*, but due to the limits of the human brain no systems are currently in use in the casinos with a *playing efficiency* in excess of 69 percent. Therefore when comparisons are made it would be more meaningful to the average player if betting efficiency were listed as a percentage of the 100 percent possible, and playing efficiency listed as a percentage of the 69 percent possible.

Most schedules that list expected advantage are misleading as they do not list the conditions required for the particular advantage. These conditions include betting spread, number of cards dealt, number of decks, and number of players. Small changes in these conditions can cause large fluctuations in expected value. Lawrence Revere quoted an advantage of from 3.2 to 4.2 percent for his advanced point-count system. When questioned by Julian Braun he explained that obtaining this advantage required the very best rules and a single-deck game dealt down to the last card. Of course such a game is never available.

Another consideration in selecting a counting system is the type of game you usually will be playing. If you expect to be playing mostly single-deck games you will be concerned with playing efficiency, and you will want to learn a wide range of variations to the basic strategy. If your game will be multi-deck, you will be primarily interested in betting efficiency and you will be able to use a much lower number of playing variations.

There are two reasons for counting cards: to determine when to increase your bet before every hand, and to determine when to vary basic strategy whenever the count is high enough. The accuracy of a counting system in locating favorable betting situations is indicated by its betting efficiency. The effectiveness of the system's ability to pinpoint when basic strategy should be changed is shown by its playing efficiency.

The value of any counting system is in direct proportion to the number of decks used. In a single-deck game, the running count is divided by the fraction of the deck remaining. This has the effect of multiplying the running count. However, in a multi-deck game, the running count is divided by the number of remaining decks, and this has the effect of dividing the running count.

Because the average true count will be lower in a multi-deck game, the range of bet sizes will also tend to be lower, but a calculation of the true count will still be required much of the time the count is positive. The effect of lower average true counts also reduces the opportunities for strategy variations, and this is closely related to the number of decks in use.

Analysis of Possible Values of a True Count of Ten

Number of Decks Played	True Count Four-Deck Game	True Count Six-Deck Game
½	2.9	1.8
1	3.3	2.0
1½	4.0	2.2
2	5.0	2.5
2½	6.7	2.9
3	10.0	3.3
3½	—	4.0
4	—	5.0
4½	—	6.7

The above table shows that going from a four-deck to a six-deck game reduces the average true count by about half, and therefore the possibilities of making a playing variation decline by a similar amount. The table also clearly indicates that the value of the counting systems with high *playing* efficiencies goes down as the number of decks goes up. In contrast, the value of systems with high *betting* efficiencies tends to remain constant.

The systems included in Exhibit 10 are limited to those I know are being successfully used in the casinos today. I have eliminated those systems that do not provide for a true count to be used for both betting and playing since they would limit the student's growth to the intermediate level. Where several systems use identical count values, I have selected the ones with the most complete true-count playing strategies. The systems are divided into three levels; these level numbers are an excellent indicator of the complexity of the system. The lower the level number the easier the system is to learn and use. Also shown are effective betting and playing efficiencies, advantages for selected one- and six-deck games, and the cost of the system.

The systems in Exhibit 10 are listed first by level with an ace side count; then all Level 1 systems are listed without an ace side count.

The efficiency numbers were extracted from *The Theory of Blackjack* by Peter A. Griffin. Betting efficiency numbers are adjusted for the ace side count. Playing efficiency numbers are adjusted as a percent of a possible 69 percent.

All the advantage numbers were computed with a formula from Arnold Snyder's *Blackjack Formula*. The one-deck game has a 50 percent cut, a one-to-four spread, Las Vegas Strip rules, and a single player. The six-deck game with Atlantic City rules and a full table has *A:* 35

Exhibit 10:
Comparison of Approved Advanced Point-Count Systems

System	Level	Adjusted Playing Efficiency	Betting Efficiency	Advantage One-Deck	Advantage Six-Deck A	B	Latest Price
with ace side count							
Canfield Expert	1	90%	95%	1.13	1.27	1.15	$ 10.00
DHM Professional	1	83	93	1.08	1.24	1.11	$195.00
High-Low Braun	1	88	97	1.13	1.28	1.18	$ 12.95
Wong	1	88	97	1.13	1.28	1.18	$ 19.95
Hi-Opt I	1	89	95	1.12	1.27	1.15	$ 14.95
Canfield Master	2	97	99	1.18	1.31	1.23	$250.00
Hi-Opt II	2	97	99	1.18	1.31	1.23	$200.00
R & T	2	91	97	1.14	1.29	1.19	$ 10.00
Uston APC	3	100	99	1.19	1.31	1.23	$ 14.95
Wong Halves	3	97	100	1.19	1.32	1.24	$ 19.95
Revere APC 1973	4	95	99	1.17	1.31	1.22	$200.00

no ace side count

Canfield Expert	90%	88%	1.07	1.21	1.05
DHM Professional	83	86	1.02	1.18	1.01
High-Low	74	97	1.08	1.26	1.15
Hi-Opt I	89	88	1.06	1.21	1.05
Uston Advanced Plus Minus	79	95	1.09	1.25	1.13

percent cut, six-to-one-spread, and surrender; *B:* 25 percent cut, ten-to-one spread, and no surrender. These variables represent some average conditions. An eight-deck game with a 50 percent cut would have a reduced advantage.

All the advantages would be nearly uniformly raised or lowered if the spread, rules, percent cut, number of players, and/or number of decks were changed. The fluctuations in advantage due to playing conditions are almost always more significant than advantage variations between different counting systems.

The comparisons in Exhibit 10 reveal that a limit is reached in attempting to increase the player's expectation of winning. The development of more complex and sophisticated blackjack strategies, then, does not noticeably increase the player's advantage over the use of simple but comprehensive point-count systems. This conclusion is confirmed by Griffin, who has evaluated various count systems and found little difference in player expectation among them. Using an advanced strategy may actually decrease the player's odds since the chance for error will be greater.

Stanford Wong's practical experience suggests that this limit may be around a 1.5 percent player advantage. He suggests certain enhancements that allow the player to exceed this upper limit. Examples are

• expand the point-count range for strategy variations (-3 to $+10$)

• modify the High-Low count itself to provide a closer

Level of Play vs. Player Advantage

Type of System Used	Estimated Player Advantage	Estimated Average Hourly Expected Profit (Betting $5 to $40)
Basic Strategy	−0.4	−$ 2.40
High Count with Simplified Basic Strategy	0.3	$ 1.80
Level 1 Point-Count with running-count betting	1.2	$ 7.20
with true-count betting	1.4	$ 8.40
with variations to basic strategy	1.5	$ 9.00

Six-deck Atlantic City game without Surrender
Average bet size—$10.00
Hands per hour—60
Number of players—7

approximation to the actual card values (use a higher-level point-count)

• use a side ace count to adjust the true count

• keep a side count of tens for use in the insurance decision

• select a more advantageous game

Obviously, each of these refinements will add to the player's work. Using all of them together would almost require access to a high-speed computer! Again, the reader must decide what level of commitment he is willing to make to the game. The greater the commitment, the higher the rewards. The table below shows this relationship in terms of the level of play versus the estimated player advantage and the average hourly expected profit. The computation of the average hourly expected profit is discussed in Chapter 14.

CONCLUSIONS AND RECOMMENDATIONS

A comparison of the player advantages for both the one-deck and the six-deck game clearly shows how little difference there is among all the approved complete advanced point-count systems. I suggest, therefore, that the only bases for selection of any system should be

• price

- ease of learning

- flexibility

Before Stanford Wong first offered *Professional Black-jack* in 1977 for $6.95, you could not buy a complete advanced point-count system for much less than two hundred dollars. Since then, in addition to Wong, Braun, Humble, and Uston have all published complete systems for under twenty dollars. Exhibit 10 lists eleven excellent advanced point-count systems; however, because of the minute differences in the advantages, any system costing from nearly a hundred dollars to over two hundred dollars can be eliminated.

It is conceded by all the recognized experts that the Level 1 systems are by far the easiest to learn and use. In *The Theory of Blackjack,* Peter A. Griffin states, "Numerical errors . . . probably occur far more often than people believe, particularly with the more complex point counts. . . . The beauty of the simple values like plus one, minus one, and zero is that they amount to mere recognition of cards with counting, rather than arithmetic, to continuously monitor the deck."

Inasmuch as Level 1 systems with an ace side count compare favorably with all the advanced systems, Levels 2, 3, and 4 systems—because of the additional complexity— also can be eliminated for all but the most dedicated player, who is determined to attain that last iota of advantage.

Using the true count for optimal betting is several times more valuable to the player than using the true count for variations to the basic strategy. Advanced counting systems giving the ace a value of -1 are among the highest in betting efficiency, and those without a side count of aces are by far the easiest of systems to learn and use. Of the four remaining approved systems, the High-Low appears to have the greatest flexibility. At the basic level it can be used to bet with the running count. As the student becomes more proficient, he can add the true count—first for optimal betting, and subsequently for precise playing decisions. Finally, adding a side count of aces, provided for in Stanford Wong's High-Low strategy, would result in a system that is the optimum balance between ease of play and maximum advantage. Because of this versatility, I recommend High-Low to all blackjack players, from intermediate to professional.

10

How to Become an Advanced Player: A Step-by-Step Approach

This chapter consolidates all of the recommendations I have previously made and presents them first as stages of evolution and second as a series of action items for those readers who intend to become students of the game. I have also estimated the time commitment for each action item. All of this information is presented in Exhibits 11 and 12.

Some people, with the help of a library of good books, have taught themselves how to become advanced and professional blackjack players. The books I recommend can be found in Chapter 18. For putting together a home library, the reader will find the books available from:

The Gambler's Book Club
630 South 11th Street
Box 4115
Las Vegas, Nevada 89106
(702) 382-7555

A basic library including all the books cited in Chapter 18 should cost no more than a hundred dollars.

Most serious students have found that learning in a structured environment is much faster and more efficient than trying to learn from books. This can be accomplished by taking a blackjack course, either at a school or by mail. Currently available courses are analyzed and evaluated in Chapter 18.

Exhibit 11:
Stages of Evolution from Beginning Player to Advanced Player

Simplified Basic Strategy

High-Count used with Simplified Basic Strategy

Basic Strategy

Level 1 Point-Count used with Basic Strategy

True Count used for Optimal Betting

True Count used for Strategy Variations from -2 to $+3$

True Count used for Strategy Variations from -2 to $+7$

Enhancements

Exhibit 12:
Action Items for the Student of the Game

No.	Action Item	Time Commitment (hours)
1	Select a learning method.	
2	Learn the basic strategy perfectly.	10
3	Practice the basic strategy so you can apply it without even thinking about it.	20
4	Learn a Level 1 point-count system. Practice it with the basic strategy.	10
5	Continue practicing at home. Keep records of your home practice sessions until you are convinced that you are playing well enough to make money playing blackjack.	30
6	Learn a betting method that will help you avoid detection, maximize your chances of winning, and minimize your risk of ruin.	10
7	Get some actual playing experience. Use a one-to-eight betting spread for the Atlantic City and Nevada Shoe Games.	30

No.	Action Item	Time Commitment (hours)
8	Learn how to use the true count together with an optimal betting method. Use chips in your home practice sessions, making and paying off bets.	20
9	Learn the true-count strategy variations in the following order: • −1 to +1 variations (occur most often) • −2 to +3 variations • −2 to +7 variations Practice at home until you can apply this technique perfectly.	30
10	Practice using the true count until you are positive you can do it perfectly. Your home records should reflect the 1.0 to 1.5 percent theoretical advantage.	30
11	Get some more casino experience. Come home a winner. Using optimal betting, get as much casino experience as you can to convince yourself that playing blackjack can be profitable.	50
12	Increase your betting scale to whatever you can afford and still bet optimally.	

13   Add enhancements in the following order:

- Side count of aces for insurance purposes.   10
- Side count of aces for precision play.   10
- Basic strategy variations for a wider range of numbers.   10
- A more complicated but more precise point-count system, Level 2 or 3. I recommend Wong Halves because it is a natural extension of High-Low. The ace is valued at −1, only four card values are different, and most of the playing variation numbers are the same.   50

Perhaps you have been adding up the time commitment hours. Don't be dismayed by the total. Learning to play blackjack with professional instruction, either in a class or by mail, will substantially reduce the time required to reach any level of proficiency desired; see Chapters 17 and 18.

11

Applying Blackjack Systems to Casino Play

The technology of blackjack playing systems and card-counting systems has mushroomed over the last fifteen years. Until recently, the focus was on optimum playing strategies, point-count systems, playing strategy variations with the point count, and the computation of an optimum bet size as a function of the point count. During the last five years, considerable practical research has been directed toward the application of this available blackjack technology. But the casinos have also been busy, developing countermeasures against each of these tools of winning blackjack. The player's objective now is to capitalize on this wealth of data and apply it in the casinos without getting barred from play.

Considerable literature has appeared regarding the application of blackjack system strategies to actual casino play. My comment on this literature will be related to the following areas:

• bet size

• return on investment

• card counting

• avoiding detection

• cheating

• selecting the optimal game

BET SIZE

The player is confronted with two dilemmas in increasing his bet size when he has the advantage: (1) determining the proper amount in relation to his total bankroll and the desired return on investment; (2) betting an amount that will not attract the attention of the casinos; e.g., if the player is betting $2 on a negative deck and then bets $20 as soon as the deck turns positive, the casino may immediately suspect that he is a counter. Some conservative players let the count determine their bet size and never make a bet larger than 1 percent of their total bankroll or more than four times their minimum bet. More aggressive players bet with the running count, as much as twelve times their minimum bet, and as high as 2 percent of their total bankroll. Naturally the more aggressive player has a higher chance of going broke. The player should understand that the odds fluctuate and he may lose during many sessions or trips before his edge prevails. With a bankroll of $2,000, betting with the true count, and never betting more than $20, the player will virtually never go broke, assuming that he is playing the system perfectly (i.e., if true count is a minus value, bet $5; if the count is a plus value, bet $10 or $20, or an amount scaled to the true count).

Stanford Wong describes an optimum approach for determining the bet size. He never plays in a game where he does not have the advantage. He watches a few hands at a table where the dealer has just shuffled. If the deck turns positive, he sits down. As soon as it turns negative, he gets up and leaves the table. This approach, while extremely effective, is not one that the average player will adopt. In my view, this would certainly detract from the fun of playing. However, if a player is serious about blackjack and wants to become one of the select few who makes a living from the game, then I recommend that he consider this approach.

There is an optimum approach for determining the bet size. It involves the classic gambler's ruin problem: how much to bet without going broke. Solution: The player should bet *in proportion* to his total bankroll an amount that corresponds to his present advantage. The approach is described by both Wong in *Professional Blackjack* and Edward O. Thorp in his article "The Kelly Money

Management System" published in the December 1979 *Gambling Times*. Optimal betting maximizes potential gain while minimizing potential risk.

RETURN ON INVESTMENT

The return on investment or the average hourly winnings are dependent on three factors:

• the player's advantage

• the average bet size

• the number of hands played per unit of time

The player's odds of winning and the bet size have been discussed previously. Let's assume, for this discussion, that the player's advantage is 1.5 percent and he is using a betting spread of $5 to $40, with an average bet of $10.

Head-to-head play against the dealer will normally yield over two hundred hands per hour. In a game with six other players, each player is dealt about sixty hands per hour. With a betting spread of $5 to $40, about $600 per hour is being invested to yield an hourly profit of $9.00. These are average figures and will occur over a period of time; short-term cycles may produce losses or higher-than-average profits.

CARD COUNTING

It is difficult to maintain an accurate card count over many hours of play. When I started I could maintain an accurate count for several hours, and after a break, I could usually play another session. I believe that most beginning blackjack players will discover similar limits of endurance. Of course today I can play much longer. During my last trip to Las Vegas I played twenty-eight hours straight without sleep and with only brief intermissions for food and other necessities. I believe there is a direct correlation between the simplicity of the system and the number of hours it can be accurately played; hence my recommendation of High-Low.

Some books recommend that the counter hold conversations with the dealer, pit boss, and other players to make the casinos think he is just another average loser. This should be attempted only to a limited extent and only for short conversations. It is very difficult to talk while actually counting. The trick is to confine the conversations to the periods when the dealer is paying off bets or shuffling cards. This is not as hard as it sounds as most players are intently watching the game while the cards are actually being dealt.

AVOIDING DETECTION

Ian Andersen's *Turning the Tables on Las Vegas* is an excellent treatise for serious blackjack players on how to avoid detection. Stanford Wong avoids detection by floating, watching for positive counts, and making flat (maximum) bets. Occasional gamblers can avoid detection by adopting a proper betting methodology as discussed above. The player who succeeds in looking like the average loser won't have any problems.

CHEATING

I don't believe that cheating is as widespread as Humble and Thorp imply in their published books. If there is any cheating, I believe it will be found in the smaller casinos in Las Vegas or around Nevada. Revere, a veteran of twenty-plus years of blackjack play, now deceased, supported my belief. Wong, a consistent winner over the years, also confirms this opinion. In his books Humble talks about a serious cheating problem in Las Vegas but presents as hard evidence published accounts of cheating in smaller Nevada communities and casinos. His other evidence would be difficult to corroborate. Nevertheless, Humble provides an excellent description of how to spot and avoid cheating dealers. I suggest the reader review this description and become familiar with the data.

SELECTING THE OPTIMAL GAME

The Blackjack Formula by Arnold Snyder provides a mathematical formula for determining the advantage of any blackjack game. It considers the betting spread, the placement of the cut card, the number of decks, and the number of players, as well as the casino rules and the counting system used. The formula can also be used to compute the variations in advantage when one of these conditions is changed. The knowledgeable blackjack player is constantly looking for the most favorable conditions.

- The betting spread is the most significant variable. Since your maximum bet is more or less fixed, you can increase your spread most easily by sitting at a lower-minimum table. Changing your spread to one-to-eight from one-to-four can improve your advantage by about 0.5 percent.

- Placing the cut card one deck instead of two decks from the end in a six-deck game will increase your edge by approximately 0.3 percent. Dealers with this cutting pattern can frequently be found in Atlantic City.

- A four-deck game will produce 0.2 percent more advantage than a six-deck game, all other conditions being identical. As this book is being written, four-deck games are offered from time to time in Atlantic City at the larger tables.

- Playing head-to-head rather than at a full table boosts your margin by about 0.1 percent. However, the improvement is multiplied because this type of game will give you many more hands per hour. Similarly, playing with faster dealers also improves your earning power.

There are several other tactics employed by more sophisticated players to enhance their earnings expectation. However, because of the fluctuating number of hands per hour, the effects are difficult to measure.

• Leaving the table when the count reaches a predetermined negative number can improve your advantage by as much as 0.5 percent. Naturally this negative number should vary according to the difficulty in finding another seat.

• Back-counting so you can sit down at a table only with a positive count and get up as soon as the deck turns negative also increases your edge but at the same time decreases the number of hands played.

• Playing two hands in positive situations is another technique for exploiting your advantage. Bet sizes should be decreased by about 30 percent to compensate for the increased risk of ruin. Casino rules may limit your ability to switch back and forth from one to two hands.

When you are taking negative walks or occasionally playing two hands you must be much more aware of observation by pit personnel. In addition, you should reduce your playing time in each pit as well as in each casino.

In his *Blackjack Formula,* Arnold Snyder says the placement of the cut card by the dealer is second in importance only to the betting spread. This would lead us to approach with caution the practice, encouraged by a number of blackjack writers, of back-counting a game already in progress, sitting down at a plus count, and adding the played but unseen cards to the decks behind the cut card. This will reduce the true count since the running count must now be divided by the remaining decks plus the played but unseen cards.

The following is an analysis of the decline in expectation as the number of played but unseen cards increases in an Atlantic City six-deck game (with Early Surrender) at a full table with a one-to-eight spread and a one-third cut.

Number of Cards Played and Not Seen	Advantage
one	1.50
½ deck	1.33
1 deck	1.18
1½ decks	1.05
2 decks	.94
2½ decks	.86
3 decks	.81
3½ decks	.78

You will note that although the decrease in advantage is sharp, your edge is never totally eliminated. The greatest danger would probably be in habitually playing in this manner rather than walking around to find a better game. That would definitely have a negative impact on overall expectation. By way of contrast, when you find a dealer who cuts one-quarter instead of one-third, the starting advantage increases from 1.50 to 1.70.

BLACKJACK TEAMS: HOW TO INCREASE YOUR WIN WITHOUT INCREASING YOUR BANKROLL

Optimal betting tables are designed to maximize the probability of doubling your bank, while at the same time minimizing the possibility of ruin. This is accomplished by raising your bet, when your advantage increases, as indicated by the count, up to the point where the advantage is exceeded by the risk of ruin to your bankroll.

Your maximum bet size, bet spread, and win rate are all therefore limited only by the size of your bankroll. To put it briefly, in order to win more you must bet more. And if you want to bet more you must have a bigger bankroll if the risk of ruin is to be kept at a minimum.

It would seem, then, that if the bank is fixed, the win rate is also fixed if the risk of ruin is to be kept constant. This is not necessarily the case. Over a period of time you could double your expected win by playing twice as long as usual, without affecting the risk of ruin. If you were able and if it were permitted, you could play at two tables simultaneously and double your expected win by playing twice as fast. It is obvious that playing twice as long or twice as fast has no effect on the risk of ruin to your bankroll, provided that you are constantly adjusting your bet size and spread to the size of your bankroll.

Instead of your playing at the second table, someone else of equal ability could play the hands for you with your bankroll, provided each of you was aware at all times when the amount jointly won or lost would change the bet sizes. It also follows that if your partner matched your bank, each of you could double your betting scale and thereby double each player's win expectation. Similarly if a third person matched the bank contribution, the betting scale and win expectation could be tripled; with four it would quadruple, and so on. The key is communication. Each player must know at all times when the total amount jointly won or lost is sufficient to change the bet sizes. As long as communication is maintained it is not necessary for team members to play at the same casino or even at the same time. The chart on page 146 is an example of the difference between individual and team betting.

Because of the greatly increased rate of bankroll fluctuation, team players should normally avoid playing at the same table. However, in addition to the mandatory signals showing amounts won or lost, team members should have a call-in signal, such as touching an ear, indicating a predetermined plus count. A teammate seeing this signal would sit down at the same table. The signaling player would then indicate the count, perhaps by handling his chips, and the second player would leave the table at the end of the shoe. While two team players are at the same table, all bet sizes are reduced by 30 percent.

Another effective team play concept is the "Big Player" or BP routine. In this program several team members play at the smallest tables available with frequent vacant seats, keeping the count and making minimum bets. The BP wanders around watching for a call-in signal and thereupon sits down and makes maximum bets, leaving the table when the count drops. A more sophisticated version of this routine has the BP paying no attention to

Casino Bankroll	Range of Bets	Playing Bankroll	Stop Loss	Estimated Per Hour
One player $ 800	$2 to $16	$400	$200	$ 3
Two players $1,600	$2 or $3 to $32	$300 each	$200 ea.; $400 total	$ 6 each
Three players $2,400	$3 or $5 to $48	$400 each	$200 ea.; $600 total	$ 9 each
One player $1,500	$2 or $3 to $30	$750	$375	$ 5
Two players $3,000	$3 or $5 to $60	$600	$375 ea.; $750 total	$10 each
Three players $4,500	$5 or $10 to $90	$750	$375 ea.; $1,125 total	$15 each

the count or even his own hand. He bets and plays the hands strictly on signals from the counting player.

Signals should be kept simple and individual for each team. Common signals for several teams would soon be picked up by casino personnel. For instance, you may decide to indicate losing a predetermined amount by raising the fingers of the left hand to the neck; losing half the amount could be signaled by using the knuckles to touch the neck. Similarly, amounts won could be shown with the same signals given with the right hand. A signal requesting a meeting at a prearranged spot could be the touching of an elbow. A warning of unusual heat might be scratching the nose. The acknowledgment of any signal could be rubbing an eyebrow. The possibilities are endless.

Teams are ideally composed of players of comparable ability and commitment to the game, who have implicit faith and trust in each other. Each player's investment need not be the same. Unequal investments can be accommodated by dividing the win of the successful team in proportion to individual wins, hours played, and investment. The key to successful team play is communication, as all bets by every player must be based on the current common bankroll.

All avid blackjack players should seriously consider the advantages of team play. Initially the primary benefit is the opportunity of playing for much higher stakes with a corresponding increase in expected earnings. The greatest value of team play however, is the averaging-out effect on individual losing cycles. It can be proven mathematically that an expert player could play flawless blackjack steadily for six months and still be in a losing streak. While it is true that a player with an adequate bankroll who constantly adjusts his maximum bets and stop losses will not go broke, his bankroll may be reduced to the point that his earnings per hour would not be satisfactory, and the time required to recoup without refinancing would be an insurmountable obstacle to profitable play.

Usually it is not practical to consider quitting your job and becoming a full-time player, for several reasons. For at least the immediate future there will not be enough casinos in Atlantic City or sufficient casinos with favorable rules in Nevada to enable the average player to play full time without an amount of exposure that would invite barring. In addition banks on occasion are lost and others sometimes churn indefinitely without doubling. Blackjack play should include an investment that would not cause financial problems if lost, and earnings that should not effect your standard of living if delayed for a substantial period of time. For the diehard who is determined to turn pro, I recommend the advice of Peter Giles in Stanford Wong's *Blackjack Newsletter* of December 1979. "Keep working and playing in your spare time until you have $10,000 plus enough to live on for three months. If, after three months, your bankroll is less than $10,000, you should quit playing blackjack. If you have won enough [to live on] . . . for the next three months, you have a handle on the game and should keep on playing."

12

Big Names on the Blackjack Scene

Those readers who decide to approach the game seriously should recognize the big names in blackjack. Each of the men listed below (alphabetically) has made a significant contribution to the game:

IAN ANDERSEN

A practical psychologist, Ian Andersen is an active player with annual blackjack winnings of six figures plus. He is the author of several books including *Turning the Tables on Las Vegas,* the classic work on how to win without being caught. Andersen is a master at avoiding detection while being dealt a high-stakes game and at the same time living like royalty, compliments of the house. Both Stanford Wong and Ken Uston have rated Andersen as a world-class player.

JULIAN BRAUN

Computer scientist and author of *How to Play Winning Blackjack,* Julian Braun is generally acknowledged as the final authority on computer-calculated blackjack strategies. Although not a serious player, Braun's contributions to the game to date have not been equaled by any other person. The reader should remember that almost any system he decides to use will have been developed from the computer calculations of Julian Braun.

JOEL H. FRIEDMAN

A more recent member of the elite group of blackjack theoreticians, Friedman is associated with the Operations Research and Systems Analysis Department at the University of North Carolina at Chapel Hill. An active blackjack player, Joel presented "Choosing a Blackjack Game" at the fourth Conference on Gambling in 1978. In 1980 he published "Risk Averse Playing Strategies in the Game of Blackjack." These papers clearly demonstrate Friedman's qualifications as an authority on blackjack analysis.

PETER A. GRIFFIN

Peter Griffin, author, professor, and active blackjack player, was the first to statistically evaluate blackjack systems. The results of his work paralleled the computer-simulation analyses of Julian Braun. Peter's *Theory of Blackjack* is so detailed and is such a complete mathematical analysis of the game that Stanford Wong termed it an applied mathematics textbook. Indeed, the work of Arnold Snyder, as well as the work of C. R. Chambliss and T. C. Roginski, is based largely on the formulas developed by Griffin. Griffin is generally acknowledged as the foremost on the mathematics of blackjack in the world today.

LANCE HUMBLE

Humble is currently associated with International Gaming Incorporated, a marketing organization for his Hi-Opt systems, the International Blackjack Club, and a highly rated harness racing handicapping system. His book *The World's Greatest Blackjack Book,* written with Carl Cooper, is an excellent textbook on blackjack and contains a complete description of Hi-Opt I. He also teaches a gambling course in a Canadian university. Many of his students have become blackjack players. Lance is still an active blackjack player.

LAWRENCE REVERE

Before his death in 1977, Revere spent about half his time playing blackjack throughout the world. He was barred from most, if not all, of the Nevada casinos. The other half of his time was spent in his Las Vegas residence, where he offered private lessons to serious students. At the time of his death, Revere was probably the most successful of all the professional blackjack players. Although some of his work is now out of date, his advanced counting system is still used on the professional level by such players as Ken Uston. A pioneer in the training of blackjack players, Lawrence Revere was the first to use color charts as a learning aid, the first to offer variable, multi-deck strategies, and the first to develop "casino comportment."

ARNOLD SNYDER

The newest and currently the most prolific analyst in today's blackjack world is Arnold Snyder. In 1980 he published *The Blackjack Formula,* containing a method for determining the player's advantage for any set of rules and conditions in any casino in the world. A simplified means of using this formula was presented in his second book, *Blackjack for Profit.* Also published in 1980 was his paper "Algebraic Approximations of Optimal Blackjack Strategy." Snyder's latest literary effort is a quarterly newsletter, *Blackjack Forum,* which promises to be on the same high level as his previous work.

EDWARD O. THORP

The casino's advantage in blackjack was substantially eliminated by the development of the correct basic strategy. Although the initial work was done by Baldwin, Cantey, Maisel, and McDermott, Dr. Thorp refined their analysis through the use of high-speed computers, and was the first to investigate what the playing strategy should be as the composition of the deck changed. He reported his findings, together with the first workable counting system, in *Beat the Dealer,* published in 1962. This best-selling classic tipped the advantage significantly in favor of the knowledgeable player.

KEN USTON

Uston is the "Big Player" who led a team of blackjack players to a one-million-dollar profit from the Las Vegas blackjack tables. He is currently embroiled in a legal battle concerning his rights to play in those casinos that have barred him, and it is likely that these legal battles will drag on for years. Widely known and seldom allowed to play in the United States, Ken publishes a bi-monthly newsletter and also offers blackjack seminars. Uston's most recent book, *Million-Dollar Blackjack,* includes two complete advanced counting systems developed by him as well as a wealth of information for every level of blackjack player.

STANFORD WONG

A true blackjack professional, playing with impunity all over the world, Stanford Wong makes his living playing blackjack and shares his expertise and knowledge through his monthly newsletters. He is a computer scientist and an innovator. Each of his books, *Professional Blackjack, Winning Without Counting,* and *Blackjack in Asia,* contains significant advances in blackjack state-of-the-art. Wong was the first to offer a complete advanced blackjack system for less than twenty dollars and held nothing back for additional fees. His strategy of never playing a negative deck has been used by countless counters since *Professional Blackjack* was first published in 1977.

PART IV

RECOMMENDED SOURCES of CASINO GAMING SERVICES

13

WHERE TO GET BLACKJACK INFORMATION

BOOKS

There is a multitude of books available on blackjack—nearly fifty that I know of. The neophyte blackjack player is presented with a mass of confusion as he attempts to select those books that will help him improve his game.

If you are interested in pursuing your study of blackjack, then here are the first books in addition to my book—*Blackjack's Winning Formula*—that I recommend you purchase (listed in alphabetical order):

Beat the Dealer by Edward O. Thorp
(Vintage Books; New York; 1966; pb $2.95)

This book originated the theory of card counting and is a must for all serious blackjack players.

Blackjack for Profit by Arnold Snyder
(R. G. Enterprises; Berkeley, CA; 1981; pb $9.95)
Blackjack for Profit is essentially written as a guide for those who are already card counters. Although it contains no strategy or counting system, it does have a "profit index" that shows at a glance which games to play and which tables to avoid. The index proves that half the available blackjack games cannot be beaten by card counting. Snyder's opinions concerning bankroll requirements and profit potential are ultra-conservative and would tend to discourage most players. His analysis of card counting systems, however, parallels in many respects the conclusions drawn in this book.

Blackjack Your Way to Riches by Richard Albert Canfield
(Expertise Publishing Co.; Scottsdale, AZ; 1977; hc $10.00)
Fascinating reading for the novice player. The win-rate expectations are overstated. Contains the Canfield Expert System.

How to Play Winning Blackjack by Julian H. Braun
(Data House Publishing Co.; Chicago; 1980; pb $12.95)
The best thing about this book is Braun's description of the basic strategy. If you are interested in why certain basic strategy plays are made, this book is for you. Highly recommended.

Million Dollar Blackjack by Ken Uston
(SRS Enterprises; Los Angeles; 1981; hc $14.95)

Ken Uston covers the blackjack scene from the occasional novice gambler to the professional team player. This makes *Million-Dollar Blackjack* probably one of the most complete books on blackjack ever published.

Playing Blackjack as a Business by Lawrence Revere
(Lyle Stuart; Secaucus, NJ; 1977; pb $9.95)

Another good book for the beginning blackjack player, with fundamental, practical advice. Contains innovative color-coded strategy tables,.

Playing Blackjack in Atlantic City by C. R. Chambliss and T. C. Roginski
(Gambler's Book Club; Las Vegas; 1981; pb $9.95)

Playing Blackjack in Atlantic City, with sixty-one charts, has more data per page and more pages per dollar (a total of 281) than any other authoritative book on blackjack. It is the most complete work to date on the mathematics of the Atlantic City multi-deck game.

Professional Blackjack by Stanford Wong
(Pi Yee Press; La Jolla, CA; 1980; hc $19.95)

Professional Blackjack is a technical book but it is required reading for the truly serious blackjack player. It contains a thorough description of the High-Low system and, for the advanced player, tables of variations of playing strategy for varying casino blackjack rules.

The World's Greatest Blackjack Book by Lance Humble and
Carl Cooper
(Doubleday & Co.; Garden City, NY; 1980; hc $14.95)
  This is a good book for beginning and intermediate
players with a lot of practical advice about blackjack.
Included is the complete Hi-Opt I system.

Turning the Tables on Las Vegas by Ian Andersen
(Vanguard; New York; 1976; pb $2.50)
  Turning the Tables on Las Vegas teaches you not how to
play blackjack but how not to get barred in the casino. Ian
Andersen is the recognized master in this technique.
Recommended reading for any serious player.

Winning Without Counting by Stanford Wong
(Pi Yee Press; La Jolla, CA; 1978; hc $50.00)
  An excellent book and the first to deal with the ploy of
reading the dealer's hole card—legitimately, without
cheating. This information cannot be used where the
dealer does not check his hole card for blackjack.

  The next four books will not help you learn how to play
blackjack, but for the student of the game who insists on
knowing "why" as well as "how," these books present the
information needed for a complete understanding of the
theory of the game.

The Blackjack Formula by Arnold Snyder
(R. G. Enterprises; Berkeley, CA; 1980; pb $100.00)
  This book contains a detailed formula for determining
the precise advantage for any blackjack game anywhere in

the world. Snyder also offers a down-to-earth discussion on standard deviation and the risks faced by the blackjack player. A high price, but well worth it to the avid player.

The Casino Gambler's Guide, enlarged edition, by Allan N. Wilson
(Harper & Row; New York; 1966; hc $11.95)

Published in 1966, this book is still considered one of the best on casino gambling odds. Wilson's work on bet sizing and the problem of gamblers' ruin is the basis of many subsequent "scientific" betting systems.

The Theory of Blackjack, revised edition, by Peter A. Griffin
(Gambler's Book Club; Las Vegas; 1981; pb $9.95)

Although much of the book is directed to those having university-level training in advanced mathematics, the serious player will find information he needs and can use. This book is considered an extension of the work of Thorp, Wilson, and Epstein.

The Theory of Gambling and Statistical Logic by Richard A. Epstein
(Academic Press; New York; 1977; hc $29.00)

An excellent treatise on the mathematics of blackjack and other gambling games. Epstein shows how gambling provides both the impetus and the only concrete base for the early development of probability theory. His analysis of gambling fallacies associated with superstition and intuitive logic is a highlight of the book.

NEWSLETTERS*

In addition to a reference library, the budding black-jack player will require up-to-date information concerning current developments in the game as well as in the casinos. You may want to consider the following:

Blackjack Forum by Arnold Snyder, $10 per year—4 issues (R. G. Enterprises, 2000 Center Street #1067, Berkeley, CA 94704)

Judging by the initial issue, *Blackjack Forum* is a welcome addition to the blackjack newsletter field. Arnold Snyder, author of *The Blackjack Formula,* offers material that is fresh and unique. At this price you cannot afford to be without it.

Casino Connection Newsletter by Steve Venture, $15 per year—6 issues
(Steve Venture, 4001 East Fanfol, Phoenix, AZ 85028)

This is a five page publication featuring articles on casino games and shows.

Rouge et Noir News by Walter Tyminski, $40 per year—approx. 10 issues
(Rouge et Noir, Inc., P.O. Box 6, Glen Head, NY 11545)

This is a newsletter devoted to the world of casino

---

*As this book goes to press, *Gambling Times* magazine plans to publish a blackjack newsletter entitled *The Experts*.

gaming. It contains many excellent articles on blackjack from a number of different perspectives: blackjack systems and book evaluations; card counters and their legal problems with getting barred (especially in Atlantic City); casino win-rates and casino policies and procedures. Readers who wish to stay abreast of the casino industry should consider subscribing to this publication. It is well worth the price.

The International Blackjack Club by Lance Humble, $24 per year—4 issues
(International Gaming Inc., Box 73, Thornhill, Ontario, Canada L3T 3N1)

This club is dedicated to reporting blackjack playing conditions throughout the world, but is primarily focused on the Nevada casinos. Members report their winnings, losings, casino rules, and suspected incidents of cheating. Humble reviews the reports, evaluates them and publishes the results in a quarterly newsletter.

Ken Uston's Blackjack Newsletter by Ken Uston, $30 per year—6 issues
(Uston Institute; P.O. Box 1949; Philadelphia, PA 19107)

Written in a breezy manner by Ken himself, this newsletter identifies new developments, rules changes and timely topics. Subscribers may send questions concerning blackjack for Ken or a member of his team to answer. Up to five questions per subscription are allowed.

Stanford Wong's Blackjack Newsletter by Stanford Wong
(Pi Yee Press; Box 1144; La Jolla, CA 92038)

Started in April, 1979, this leader in the field has subsequently been subdivided into three separate publications. I think very highly of all three letters. They are an excellent value for both the professional and occasional player. These newsletters contain tips on blackjack, answer reader questions, and publish very interesting letters from blackjack professionals all around the world.

Current Blackjack News $95 per year—12 issues
—features the latest information of new casinos, casino promotions, and rules changes. A highlight is the continual evaluation of all United States casinos, showing number of blackjack tables, casino edge, number of decks, and comments both good and bad. The blackjack player who travels would be lost without this information.

Nevada Blackjack $21 per year—6 issues
—contains articles with a Nevada flavor. There are fascinating articles from time to time by Peter Giles, possibly the most effective blackjack player in action today.

Blackjack World $21 per year—6 issues
—covers Atlantic City and contains articles of interest to blackjack players throughout the world. Here is where you will find a continual evaluation of all casinos outside the United States.

MAGAZINES

Gambling magazines, in general, cover the whole gambling spectrum from horse racing to casino games. The following, from time to time, contain information on blackjack:

Boardwalker $1.75 per copy, $9.75 per year—9 issues
(2515 Pacific Avenue, Atlantic City, NJ 08041)
Contains articles on a variety of subjects, including blackjack. The emphasis is on Atlantic City. Well worth the price.

Casino & Sports $3 per copy, $15 per year—5 issues
(Gambler's Book Club, Box 4115, Las Vegas, NV 89106)
This periodical is dedicated to reviewing and evaluating systems and methods for all casino games. Those readers wanting updates and data on the latest blackjack systems should subscribe to this publication. I recommend it.

Casino Times $.50 per copy, $5 per year—12 issues
(1516 Atlantic Avenue, Atlantic City, NJ 08401)
This is a newspaper covering the Atlantic City casino scene. In addition to articles on blackjack, it has many ads for gambling casinos.

Chips $2.95 per copy, $15 per year—6 issues
(49 West 45th Street, New York, NY 10036)
This is a new entry in the field. A slick publication containing gambling articles and ads.

Gambling Gazette $1.65 per copy, $15 per year—12 issues (Casino Research Services, Box 47, Atlantic Highlands, NJ 07716)

Items on casino and other gambling with many ads.

Gambling Scene $1.25 per copy, $12 per year—13 issues (Box 669, Mountain View, CA 94042)

Contains articles on blackjack and other forms of gambling. Specializes in poker as it is played in California card rooms.

Gambling Times $2.95 per copy, $29 per year—12 issues (1018 N. Cole Avenue, Hollywood, CA 90038)

Contains columns, ads, and articles on all types of gambling. Publishes many gambling systems. The oldest surviving gaming magazine.

Gaming Business $6 per copy, $65 per year—12 issues (BMT Publications Inc., 2nd floor, 254 W 31 St., New York, NY 10001)

A management-oriented magazine with articles on all phases of the gambling business. Contains financial information on casinos and news on casinos yet to open.

Gaming and Travel Digest $4 per copy, $35 per year—12 issues (Behavioral Learning Center, Box 160856, Miami, FL 33116)

Slanted toward junkets and air travel. Contains articles and ads on gambling.

Million$ $2 per copy, $18 per year—12 issues
(Million$ Magazine Subscription Dept., Box 6722 Postal
Station A, Toronto, Ontario, Canada M5W 1X5)

Features articles on speculative investments. Contains
articles and ads on blackjack and other forms of gambling.

Systems & Methods $3 per copy, $15 per year—6 issues
(Gambler's Book Club, Box 4115, Las Vegas, NV 89106)

Before *Casino & Sports* was split off, this magazine
covered the whole gambling spectrum. S & M now
concentrates on parimutuel betting sports.

BLACKJACK SCHOOLS

Of all the sources of blackjack information, the growth
in the number of blackjack schools and courses has been
the most spectacular. There are currently twelve schools
offering lessons in basic strategy, card counting, and
money management. The costs go from a low of $195 to a
high of $695; the time required ranges from four to
sixteen hours; and the length of the courses varies from
one day to six weeks.

Since the price of a blackjack course amounts to
considerably more than any other source of information,
the student who insists on maximum value for his money
must be wary. In addition to cost, the paramount consid-
erations are the expertise, experience, and reputation of
the instructor; the quality and completeness of the system
taught; and, finally and most important, the organization
of the material and how it is presented.

There is very little taught in any blackjack school that is not available in books costing a fraction of the price of the course. Similarly, the library in any good university contains all of the information one needs to become a doctor, a lawyer, or an accountant. The problem is, of course, that few people can efficiently teach themselves with just a book. Learning is easiest in a structured environment with lectures, reading assignments, drills, practice sessions, and quizzes, with provisions for questions from the student and answers by a qualified instructor at all stages of the learning process.

For maximum effectiveness, the progress of the student must be closely monitored by the instructor while the material is being presented; while it is actually being learned via drills and other assignments; and finally while the student is demonstrating his grasp of all the material taught through quizzes and/or practice sessions in class. For the vast majority of students this is accomplished best in a time frame that provides for practicing, as well as learning, each phase of the course.

I strongly believe that the material should not be presented faster than the average person can absorb and learn to use it. Large amounts of material, regardless of quality, offered in concentrated periods of time are little more effective than textbooks alone for most people. Beware of anyone who promises to teach you basic strategy, card counting, optimal betting, and casino comportment in less than a month.

The following schools, listed alphabetically, each offer a basic strategy, a card-counting system, and a money-management system:

Canfield Expertise School of Winning Blackjack
Sacramento, CA
$200, eight hours of instruction, taught in one day
   An abbreviated course offered by the authors of
Blackjack Your Way to Riches, who teach their own counting
system, the Canfield Expert Count.

Casino Gambling Workshop
P.O. Box 562, Toms River, NJ 08753
$300, twelve hours of instruction, taught over four weeks
   Henry J. Tamburin teaches the High-Low counting
system in classes scheduled from time to time as students
indicate interest.

Darwin Ortiz Gambling School
34-57 82 St., Suite 4G, Jackson Heights, NY 11372
$300, twelve hours of instruction, taught over six weeks
   Blackjack for the Analytical Gambler using the ITA counting system is one of the courses offered by Ortiz, who is
no longer an active player. The other two are *Craps for the
Fast Action Gambler* and *General Strategies of Six Casino
Games for the Recreational Player.* The school appears to be
aimed at the gambler and recreational player.

International School of Blackjack
1228 Delaware Ave., Cherry Hill, NJ 08002
$375, twelve hours of instruction, taught over four days
   Robert and Judy Jamerson teach the Canfield Expert
Count. Regular classes are offered, but students are urged
to take semi-private instruction (two students) for an extra
$50. This course is too concentrated for most players.

Jerry Patterson's Blackjack Clinic
One Britton Place, Voorhees, NJ 08043
$450, fifteen hours of instruction taught over five weeks

This school features the complete High-Low system in three separate courses for the basic to intermediate, advanced, or professional player. In addition, all the material is offered in a correspondence-course format for those who find it impractical to attend classes offered in the New York or Southern California, New Jersey, Philadelphia, Baltimore/Washington areas, or for the student who desires to learn over a longer period of time. The price includes complete and continuous followup services. Complete details can be found in Chapter 14.

Professional School of Winning Blackjack
14 Route 73, Marlton, NJ, and
315 Route 46, Rockaway, NJ
$495, twelve hours of instruction, taught over three days

Vivian Bush and Ralph Stricker teach the Gold-Plus Count. This is the Roberts count balanced by valuing the ace as 0. Bush and Stricker formerly operated the *Stanley Roberts School of Winning Blackjack* in Marlton, NJ. The advertising for the course presents unrealistic claims and the instruction is given in too brief a period of time.

Scientific Systems Inc.
2705 Black Road, Joliet, IL 60435
$695, twenty hours of instruction, taught over three days

The Roberts Count is taught in a highly concentrated course. This school operates out of Illinois but schedules classes in many cities all over the United States. Their advertising appears to offer unsubstantiated win probabilities.

Seminar 21
9 S. Kentucky Ave., Atlantic City, NJ 08041
$195, eighteen hours of instruction, taught over two weeks
   Tim Hamilton teaches the High-Low counting system, money management, and casino comportment.

S & S Gaming Institute, aka *Golden Eagle Gaming Institute*
8400 Bustleton Ave. Suite 301, Philadelphia, PA 19115
$650, fourteen hours of instruction, taught over seven weeks
   Doug Grant teaches a noncounting system that contradicts all known winning blackjack theory. The student is instructed to watch for card patterns indicating situations when the bet should be raised or playing strategy changed. Not recommended.

Stanley Roberts School of Winning Blackjack
1018 N. Cole Ave., Hollywood, CA 90038
$595, sixteen hours of instruction, taught over four days
   This school, located in California, also offers courses in a number of cities throughout the United States. The Roberts 10-count system is taught.

Uston Institute of Blackjack
P.O. Box 1949, Philadelphia, PA 19107
$495, four to six hours of instruction, taught in one day
   Ken Uston or one of his teammates teaches the Uston

Advanced Plus Minus in a semiprivate class (three to five students). The Uston Advanced Point Count is also presented. Ken offers to show students of other counting systems how to become competent card counters. For the serious student of the game, the opportunity of spending half a day with the acknowledged master of blackjack makes the class a worthwhile investment.

In addition to the caveats listed above, the student is advised to be especially wary of unrealistic promises. It is generally acknowledged by the theoreticians of the game (Braun, Griffin, Snyder, and Wong, to name just a few) that your *average* advantage with an efficient counting system, accurately played, will not exceed 1.5 percent. There is also general agreement that no one can win almost all of the time. You should win more than you lose and, in the long run, an effective player should win approximately 150 percent of all the money he bets. Beware of anyone who promises any more.

LEARNING AIDS

There are several new ways to learn to play winning blackjack. The costs range from less than twenty-four dollars to two hundred dollars. I suggest that you thoroughly investigate and evaluate these learning tools before you buy:

Audio Cassettes

• *Winning Blackjack: The Easy Way*
  Cassette or recording, $15 plus $1 p/h
  Jim Jasper
  J & W Recording Co., Box 2A, 676 N. LaSalle,
  Chicago, IL 60610

• *Blackjack: Your Own Professional Program*
  Four tapes with flashcards and booklet, $39.95 plus
  $1.50 p/h
  Darwin Ortiz
  TP Publishing Co., 201 East 28 St.,
  New York, NY 10016

Video Cassettes

• *Professional Blackjack Winning Techniques*
  Betamax or VHS, 2 hours, $49.95
  Instructional Video Cassette Corporation, 2035 S. 7 St.,
  Philadelphia, PA 19148

• *Beat the House at Blackjack*
  Betamax or VHS, 2 hours, $59.95
  Ken Uston
  Uston Institute, P.O. Box 1949, Philadelphia, PA 19107

• *Las Vegas and Atlantic City Blackjack*
  Betamax or VHS, 3 hours, $99 plus $4 p/h
  Howard Grossman, 800 Langtry Drive,
  Las Vegas, NV 89107

Slides

• *Slides to Learn Basic Strategy and How to Count*
  140 Slides, $130
  Dobratz Enterprises, Inc., P.O. Box 19243,
  Las Vegas, NV 89119

The lack of a provision for interaction between the teacher and the student is the major drawback of both cassettes and slides. They really only amount to a sophisticated presentation of material that can be found in a book. Perhaps a more efficient way of learning to play blackjack would be one of the computer programs reviewed next.

MICROCOMPUTER-AIDED BLACKJACK INSTRUCTION

The computer age has caught up with the individual blackjack player. This isn't to say that computers are a novelty to the game—far from it. For over twenty years, starting with Dr. Edward O. Thorp—who published the first successful counting system in *Beat the Dealer* in 1962— high-speed computers have been busy cranking out basic strategies as well as countless counting and betting systems. Now, however, programs are available that will assist the blackjack enthusiast to learn winning strategies.

Provided that you have access to a microcomputer (costs range from around nine hundred dollars to over thirty-five hundred dollars), a computer program costing anywhere from ninety dollars to two hundred dollars can help you become an expert blackjack player. This is not the starting place for a novice. If you do not know how to play, a program will not teach you the rules of the game, basic strategy, or how to count and use the count to vary your bet or your playing strategy. But once you know the fundamentals, playing blackjack on a computer can substantially improve your skills in any of these areas.

Progressing from basic strategy to card counting and varying your betting as well as playing strategy with the count, the computer can be programmed to deal you a game requiring ever more sophisticated decisions as your level of expertise improves. These programs usually include a "tutor" function that senses the decisions you make hesitantly or incorrectly and that will automatically deal you more hands covering these situations. Most programs allow the player to practice against variable rules and playing conditions so that he can be prepared to play anywhere in the world.

If you know how to play blackjack but are not satisfied with your progress, consider practicing against a computer. A good program could enable you to reach the level of competency needed to win in the casino.

Computer-Assisted Blackjack Tutor for TRS-80 Model 3
Jerry Patterson
Echelon Enterprises,
One Britton Place,
Voorhees, NJ 08043
$90 (approx) for program, $900 for computer
Featuring the High-Low counting system, this program will allow you to play a game with any number of players,

any number of decks, any range of bet sizes, and a variable shuffle point.

The World's Greatest Blackjack Program for 48K Apple II or II Plus
Warren Irwin
CCA Associates, 1541 Froesel, Ellisville, MO 63011
$95 for program, $1,550 for computer
   This program has practice modes for practicing basic strategy, Hi-Opt I counting system, and betting with a spread of eight-to-one. It is limited to four decks and only six can play.

Expert Blackjack for Hewelett Packard HP 85
Paul Dayton
R. G. Enterprises, 2000 Center St. # 1067,
Berkeley, CA 94704
   $200 for program, $3,250 for computer
   A complete program, including basic strategy, the Canfield counting systems, and a betting spread of eight-to-one. It is limited to a head-to-head game by one player.

The Amazing Blackjack Machine for 16K Level II TRS-80 (Models I & III)
H. J. Tamburin and R. Ramm
Casino Gambling Workshops, Box 562,
Toms River, NJ 08753
$25 for program, $900 for computer
   This program will not teach you how to play blackjack. It is designed for the development, study, and analysis of blackjack playing strategies and betting systems.

Exhibit 13:
Available Computer-Assisted Blackjack Instruction Programs

	World's Greatest Blackjack Program	Expert Blackjack	Computer-Assisted Blackjack Tutor
Name of Program:	World's Greatest Blackjack Program	Expert Blackjack	Computer-Assisted Blackjack Tutor
Computer Model:	48K Apple II or II Plus	Hewlett Packard HP 85	TRS-80 Model 3
Cost of Computer:	$1,550	$3,250	Approx. $900
Cost of Program:	$95	$200	Approx. $90
Program Designer:	Carl Cooper	Paul Dayton	Jerry Patterson
Distributor:	CCA Associates 1541 Froesel Ellisville, MO 63011	R.G. Enterprises 2000 Center St. # 1067 Berkeley, CA 94704	Echelon Enterprises One Britton Place Voorhees, NJ 08043
Counting System:	Hi-Opt I	Canfield Expert/ Master	High-Low

Name of Program:	World's Greatest Blackjack Program	Expert Blackjack	Computer-Assisted Blackjack Tutor
Number of Decks:	1 to 4	Any	Any
Number of Players:	1 to 6	1	1 to 7
Maximum Bet Spread:	8-to-1	8-to-1	Any
Rules:	Any	Any	Any
Shuffle Point:	Variable	Any	Variable
Discard Display:	Yes	Yes	Yes
Running & True Count:	Yes	Yes	Planned
Ace Count:	No	Yes	No
Teaches Basic Strategy:	Yes	Yes	Yes
Teaches Counting:	Yes	Yes	Yes
Teaches Betting:	Yes	Yes	Yes

CASINO GAMING EQUIPMENT AND SUPPLIES

For the casino gamer interested in setting up his own practice and play facilities at home or at the club, there is an excellent source of gaming supplies and equipment available in the Philadelphia/South Jersey area—*Gil's Guide to Casino Gaming*.

Gil offers handsome, sturdy, foldup blackjack tables for a low discount price—$375. Comparable tables run well over $500. You may even order the table with the Atlantic City basic strategy imprinted on the layout.

Gil also offers dealer's shoes, casino-like chips, discard holders, blackjack layouts, and many other fine products, all at discount prices. Write directly to Gil for a catalogue:

Gilbert E. Stead
Gil's Guide to Casino Gaming
Dept. QP
1601 Fairhill Place
Clementon, NJ 08021
Telephone: (609) 228-7277

14

Casino Gaming Services Offered by Jerry L. Patterson

This section is promotional in nature. Because I am committed to and believe in what I am doing, I have included, in Chapter 14, a description of the casino gaming services I offer. The main service is a Blackjack Clinic in which I instruct beginning to intermediate blackjack players in the application of *Blackjack's Winning Formula*. I invite reader inquiries on this and other services. An information request form is included as the last page of this book.

THE BLACKJACK CLINIC

The BLACKJACK CLINIC is a Blackjack School I own and operate. Fifteen hours of instruction are delivered to the student over a five-week period—three hours, one night a week, for five weeks.

There are a number of unique and extraordinary features about this school. Here are just a few:

- The students actually win money (I know this because I poll them every three months).

- Anyone can learn to win because I have stripped the mystique from winning blackjack methods. (Our students come from all walks of life: insurance agents, truck drivers, construction workers, housewives, self-employed businesspeople, retired persons, etc.)

- The program is continuous—followup service includes a joint visit to a casino, an open line to me and my instructors, periodic review sessions and blackjack updates, and a blackjack newsletter.

Why, you may be asking, should I take your course on blackjack after just reading your book on blackjack? There are a number of reasons why you should consider it:

- It is difficult to learn from any book, my own included. In a book you can learn *what* winning blackjack is all about, but the key is *how*. How to play basic strategy perfectly without even thinking about it. How to count cards swiftly and accurately. How to bet to maximize your profits and minimize your chances of going broke. How to avoid getting barred.

• The keys to learning how to win are the drills and exercises. In the BLACKJACK CLINIC, there are seven basic strategy drills and nine card-counting drills. Doing these drills is easy and fun. You record your progress and gain a keen sense of accomplishment as you watch your skills develop.

• It has been proven that a person learns faster and more effectively in a classroom environment. There are only a limited number of students per class and each receives all the individual attention he or she needs from me or one of my personally trained instructors. If you need a makeup session, you get it. If you need extra help, you come in early or stay late.

• Beginning or intermediate players will especially benefit from the BLACKJACK CLINIC, although quite a few advanced students have taken it to "fine tune" their game. No one is held back and each progresses at his own rate of speed.

• Practice is extremely important. We program your home practice sessions for you while you take the CLINIC. In my opinion, it is impossible to learn winning blackjack in a weekend or on four successive nights and then go home and practice correctly with no supervision or feedback.

If you want further information, just check the appropriate box in the Request Form at the end of this section.

THE ADVANCED BLACKJACK CLINIC

Learning how to count cards and using this information to vary your bet size is all you need to know to win at blackjack. You learn this in the BLACKJACK CLINIC. Serious students of the game, who are playing semiprofessionally and desire to put the "icing on the cake," enroll in the ADVANCED CLINIC and learn to gain a small but significant (in terms of dollars won) additional advantage. The following are the highlights of the ADVANCED CLINIC, which I offer to my graduates plus other qualified students:

- You learn that the running count becomes more significant as the shoe is dealt out and the number of decks remaining to be played decreases.

- You learn to use this information to compute a true count used for basic strategy variations and more precise betting decisions.

- You learn to obtain a small but powerful additional advantage by counting aces and using this side count for making more precise insurance, strategy, and betting decisions.

- You learn about the power of team play and why the casinos fear well-trained blackjack teams.

If you wish further information, check the appropriate box on the Request Form at the end of this section.

BLACKJACK CORRESPONDENCE COURSE

Blackjack: A Winner's Handbook sold twelve thousand copies in its first two printings. The readers of this book are beginning to intermediate blackjack players from all parts of the country and from foreign countries as well. Many of them have just as much interest in learning to play blackjack the right way as students in this area. Many of the readers wrote to me asking for additional information about my Self-Instruction Course.

Because of this interest I was motivated to duplicate the BLACKJACK CLINIC for use outside my own geographic area. But it had to be done right. I had to get personally involved with each student. Because of its interactive nature, a correspondence course with telephone consultation was the only vehicle that would accomplish this objective.

The BLACKJACK CORRESPONDENCE COURSE was thus born. It has proven tremendously successful and has assisted dozens of students to become winning blackjack players. Here are the highlights:

- You can work at your own rate of speed in the privacy of your own home.

- Winning blackjack cannot be learned by reading books; you will gain invaluable practical experience before risking your money in the casinos.

- The entire body of blackjack data is presented to you in an orderly fashion to simplify the learning process.

- You are not working alone. You have access to me at all times via telephone or written correspondence.

- The skills that you will achieve are measurable and as you record your drill performance, you will see these skills increasing; e.g., you will learn to count down a single deck in less than thirty seconds.

- Once you have achieved your desired level of skills, you decide upon the winnings you want to achieve. My unique money-management methods will show you how to achieve your desired level of winnings.

- The one most-heard comment from my students is that they are impressed with my honesty, integrity, and genuine desire to develop them into accomplished, money-making blackjack players. This is why I schedule a joint visit to the casino to observe and comment on your play where it really counts—under actual casino conditions.

The BLACKJACK CORRESPONDENCE COURSE is divided into three levels and eight lessons as follows:

LEVEL I	1. The Basic Strategy
SKILLED BLACKJACK PLAYER	2. The High-Low Point-Count System
	3. Basic Money Management
	4. Casino Comportment (How not to get barred)

LEVEL II

ADVANCED BLACK-
JACK PLAYER

5. Basic Strategy
Variations with the
True Count

6. Advanced Money
Management

7. Side Count of Aces

LEVEL III

TEAM BLACKJACK
PLAYER

8. How to Multiply Your
Winnings Through
Team Play

Each lesson consists of:

- A detailed lesson plan including background information, complete instructions, assignment descriptions and a statement of the skills to be achieved

- Reading assignments

- Memory aids

- Drills—drill sheets, single-deck, and multiple-deck drills are used

- An essay assignment

- A quiz

- Questions and answers

After you complete each lesson you will send all materials to me for my written critique, which will be forwarded to you by return mail. Any out-points will be corrected and you will achieve the projected skill level before you undertake the next lesson. You may stop after achieving your desired level of play—you pay for only those lessons you decide to take.

For further information, check the appropriate box on the Request Form.

BLACKJACK CLINIC FRANCHISES

Because of the success of the BLACKJACK CLINIC in the Philadelphia/South Jersey area, I am expanding into other areas. The franchise holders I am seeking must be successful blackjack players. What better source than my own students? I have struck a profitable balance between teaching and playing that I am confident I can duplicate in other individuals in other areas, just as I have with students in this area.

One student is my full-time instructor and teaches the CLINICS in this area. Another teaches weekends in New York—he also holds a full-time job. It's pretty much up to you what you want to do.

Now here is what I can do for you.

1. I will teach you to become a skilled, then advanced, then team blackjack player through the BLACKJACK CLINIC, ADVANCED CLINIC, or the BLACKJACK CORRESPONDENCE COURSE.

2. I will present you with a BLACKJACK CLINIC Franchise Plan. This plan will show you how, *in your spare time,* you can build a successful BLACKJACK CLINIC in

your area. You and I will be partners, and I will be right there with you during the key start-up period to help you implement all of my organizational and instructional materials. Much of the marketing for your area will be done centrally—through my books and newspaper columns.

COMPUTER-ASSISTED BLACKJACK TUTOR

Custom-designed for use with the relatively inexpensive TRS-80 Model 3 computer, the *Computer-Assisted Blackjack Tutor* will enable a player with just elementary knowledge of basic strategy, card counting, and money management to become a highly skilled blackjack player. The program includes the High-Low counting system, easiest to learn, easiest to play, used by more players than any other system, and rivaling the most advanced count for efficiency.

Working at your own pace, in the privacy of your own home or office, you can gain invaluable experience and achieve any desired level of expertise before risking your money at the tables. *The Computer-Assisted Blackjack Tutor* features three types of drill and practice aids. Each is discussed below.

Basic Strategy Drills

The player can set indicators to allow him to play any kind of hand:

• The player can ask for random cards to be dealt against random dealer's up cards.

- The player can fix the dealer's up card and play random hands.

- The player can ask for pairs or double-down hands to be dealt against fixed ranges of dealer up cards.

- The player can play soft hands only against fixed or variable dealer up cards.

The computer remembers those hands that give the player problems and increases the frequency of the problem hands. Any errors are immediately corrected. The player is given a second chance to get the right answer before the computer communicates it to the player.

The player can also play a blackjack game drill and specify the number of hands to be dealt per round and the number of hands to be played by the player. The computer plays the others.

A full recap is given at the end of the session.

Card-Counting Drill and Practice

The player can have the cards shown to him at variable rates of speed. The objective is to keep the count as fast as the cards flash on the screen.

The player can play a 1-to-7-player game drill and play any or all of the hands—the computer plays the others. The player can specify the speed at which the cards are dealt and whether or not the computer will check for basic strategy.

The player can request to see the correct count at the completion of each hand.

Money-Management Drill and Practice

The player can bet one hand per round. The computer checks for a correct bet size according to a prescribed money-management formula.

See and use this program with a fully qualified instructor at my Blackjack Academy at One Britton Place, Voorhees, New Jersey, before you buy. For further information, just check the appropriate box on the Request Form at the end of this section.

OTHER SERVICES

1. *Blackjack's Winning Formula*

This is the first book I know of with the emphasis on the Atlantic City game, although I also explain how to win in Nevada and the Caribbean. An excellent primer for beginning players. You may order a copy of *Blackjack's Winning Formula* by checking the appropriate box on the Request Form.

2. Personal Consultation

I offer a limited amount of personal consultation to advanced blackjack players. In an hour or two I can help you increase your card-counting speed, select an optimal betting table geared to your profit objectives and bankroll size, and show you some memory tricks for broadening your range of basic strategy index numbers. This consultation is limited to players using the High-Low Point-Count System. As my time is expensive, I recommend that you investigate the BLACKJACK CLINIC and ADVANCED BLACKJACK CLINIC before considering personal consultation.

3. Tools of the Trade

You may order a wallet-sized copy of the basic strategy and/or a set of basic strategy flash cards. You may also order a copy of my review of eleven popular blackjack books, which appeared in the January 1979 edition of *West Coast Review of Books*.

4. Weekly Columns

As this book goes to a second printing, the following newspapers publish my weekly casino gaming column:

1. *Philadelphia Bulletin* (Tuesdays on Atlantic City page)
2. *Trentonian* (Trenton, NJ; Fridays)

The column has appeared in the following newspapers:

1. *Philadelphia Daily News*
2. *South Jersey Courier-Post*
3. *Atlantic City Press*
4. *New York Daily News* (five-part series on all casino games)
5. *San Francisco Chronicle* (ten-part series on all casino games)
6. *Baltimore Sun* (ten-part series on all casino games)
7. *Asbury Park Press* (seven-part series on blackjack)
8. *The Register* (Orange County, CA; ten-part series on all casino games)

5. *Blackjack Bulletin*

This blackjack newsletter is distributed free to graduates of my BLACKJACK CLINIC, ADVANCED CLINIC and CORRESPONDENCE COURSE. I use it to keep all my students and former students up to date on course enhancements, blackjack profit opportunities from around the world, and blackjack intelligence data (where the "heat" is and how to avoid getting barred).

Bibliography

Andersen, Ian. *Turning the Tables on Las Vegas.* New York: Vanguard, 1976.

Archer, John. *The Archer Method of Winning at 21.* Hollywood, CA: Wilshire, 1978.

Baldwin, Roger, Wilbert Cantey, Herbert Maisel, and James McDermott. "The Optimum Strategy in Blackjack." *Journal of the American Statistical Association* Vol. 51 (1956), pp. 429–439.

Braun, Julian H. *How to Play Winning Blackjack.* Chicago: Data House Publishing Co., 1980.

Canfield, Richard Albert. *Blackjack Your Way to Riches.* Scottsdale, AZ: Expertise Publishing Co., 1977.

Chambliss, C. R., and T. C. Roginski, *Playing Blackjack in Atlantic City.* Las Vegas: Gambler's Book Club, 1980.

Chin, S. Y. *Understanding and Winning Casino Blackjack.*

New York: Vantage, 1980.

Collver, Donald I. *Scientific Blackjack.* New York: Arco, 1977.

Donatelli, Dante A. *Blackjack—Total Profit Strategy.* Greenburg, PA: Mar Lee Enterprises, 1979.

Dubey, Leon J. Jr. *No Need to Count.* San Diego: A. S. Barnes & Co., 1980.

Einstein, Charles. *How to Win at Blackjack.* Las Vegas: Gambler's Book Club, 1968.

Epstein, Richard A. *The Theory of Gambling and Statistical Logic.* New York: Academic Press, 1977.

Friedman, Joel. "Choosing a Blackjack Game." Fourth Conference on Gambling, 1978.

Friedman, Joel. "Risk Averse Playing Strategies in the Game of Blackjack." Spring 1980 Operations Research Conference, 1980.

Fristedt, Bert, and David Heath. "The Most Powerful Blackjack System Ever Devised." *Winning,* 15 (May), 1977. Oakland House Publishing Co., Toronto, Canada.

Goodman, Mike. *How to Win.* New York: Holloway, 1971.

Goodman, Mike, and Michael J. Goodman. *Your Best Bet.* New York: Ballantine Books, 1977.

Gordon, E. "Optimum Strategy in Blackjack—A New Analysis." Claremont Economic Paper Number 52, January 1973. The Claremont Colleges, Claremont, California.

Griffin, Peter A. *The Theory of Blackjack.* Las Vegas: Gambler's Book Club, 1981.

Guild, Leo. *The World's Greatest Gambling System.* Los Angeles: Holloway House, 1970. Revised edition.

Gwynn, John M. Jr., and Armand Seri. "Experimental

Comparisons of Blackjack Betting Systems." Fourth Conference on Gambling, 1978.

Humble, Lance. *Blackjack Gold.* Toronto: International Gaming, 1976. Retitled *Blackjack Super/Gold,* 1979.

Humble, Lance, and Carl Cooper. *The World's Greatest Blackjack Book.* Garden City, NY: Doubleday & Co., 1980.

Ita, Koko. *21 Counting Methods to Beat 21.* Las Vegas: Gambler's Book Club, 1976.

Noir, Jacques. *Casino Holiday.* Berkeley, CA: Oxford Street Press, 1970.

Nolan, Walter I. *The Facts of Blackjack.* Las Vegas: Gambler's Book Club, 1970.

Patterson, Jerry. *Blackjack's Winning Formula.* Voorhees, NJ: Casino Gaming Specialists, 1980. Revised and expanded edition. New York: Perigee Books, 1982.

Revere, Lawrence. *Playing Blackjack as a Business.* Secaucus, NJ: Lyle Stewart, 1977.

Riddle, Major A., and Joe Hyams. *The Weekend Gambler's Handbook.* New York: Random House, 1963.

Roberts, Stanley. *How to Win at Weekend Blackjack.* Los Angeles: Scientific Research Services, 1973.

Roberts, Stanley. *Winning Blackjack.* Los Angeles: Scientific Research Services, 1971.

Rouge et Noir, staff. *Winning at Casino Gaming.* Glen Head, NY: Rouge et Noir, 1975.

Scarne, John. *Scarne's Complete Guide to Gambling.* New York: Simon and Schuster, 1961, 1974.

Silberstrang, Edwin. *Playboy's Guide to Casino Gambling, Volume Two: Blackjack.* New York: Wideview Books, 1980.

Snyder, Arnold. *The Blackjack Formula.* Berkeley, CA: R. G. Enterprises, 1980.

Snyder, Arnold. *Blackjack for Profit.* Berkeley, CA: R. G. Enterprises, 1980.

Thorp, Edward O. *Beat the Dealer.* New York: Random House, 1962. Revised version: New York: Vintage Books, 1966.

Titchkosky, Ken, and Yusef Javeri. *Better Blackjack for Business and Pleasure.* Alberta: TAJ & Associates, 1980.

Uston, Ken, and Robert Rapoport. *The Big Player.* New York: Holt, Rinehart & Winston, 1977.

Uston, Ken. *Two Books on Blackjack.* Wheaton, MD: Uston Institute of Blackjack, 1979.

Uston, Ken. *Million Dollar Blackjack.* Los Angeles: SRS Enterprises, 1981.

Wilson, Allan N. *The Casino Gambler's Guide.* Enlarged edition. New York: Harper & Row, 1977.

Wong, Stanford. *Professional Blackjack.* Las Vegas: Gambler's Book Club, 1977. Revised version: La Jolla, CA: Pi Yee Press, 1980.

Wong, Stanford. *Winning Without Counting.* La Jolla, CA: Pi Yee Press, 1978.

Wong, Stanford. *Blackjack in Asia.* La Jolla, CA: Pi Yee Press, 1979.

Appendix

A List of Blackjack Systems

This Appendix contains a list of most, if not all blackjack systems available at the time of publication. Each system is listed by name, type, and rating.

KEY

PBS	Progressive Betting Strategy
BPS	Basic Playing Strategy
RCS	Rank-Count System
TCS	Ten-Count System
NCS	Noncount System
L1PCS	Level 1 Point-Count System
L2PCS	Level 2 Point-Count System
L3PCS	Level 3 or 4 Point-Count System

US   Ultimate System
A   Approved/Acceptable
R   Recommended
NR   Not Recommended

System	Type	Rating
Accu-Count System	L2PCS	NR
Archer System	TCS	NR
Atvada Proven Method of Play	BPS	NR
Aus the Boss Blackjack System	L1PCS	NR
Austin's Starter System	L1PCS	NR
AWK Count	L2PCS	NR
Basic Blackjack Betting (Einstein, C.)	PBS	NR
Blackjack Profits	PBS	NR
Beat the Dealer Blackjack Computer	BPS	NR
Blackjack Calculator	BPS	NR
Blackjack: How to Improve Your Playing Strategy in the Game of 21	BPS	NR
Blackjack Mate	BPS	NR
Black-Jack-O-Matic	BPS	NR
Blackjack (21) Solitaire	PBS	NR
Blackjack Winning Wheel	BPS	NR
Boyd—Play Better Blackjack	L1PCS	NR
Braun High-Low	L1PCS	R
Canfield Expert	L1PCS	A
Canfield Master	L2PCS	A
Carter RPI	L1PCS	NR
Collver Advanced Casing	US	NR
Collver Scientific Blackjack	L1PCS	NR
Conklin System	L1PCS	NR
Crayne System	PBS	NR

System	Type	Rating
Dubner High-Low	L1PCS	NR
DHM Professional	L1PCS	A
DHM Expert/Ultimate	US	NR
Einstein Counting System	L1PCS	NR
Fristedt—Head System	US	NR
Goldberg Computer System	TCS	NR
Gordon System	L1PCS	NR
Greatest Revolutionary Blackjack Method	PBS	NR
Green Fountain Count Strategy	L1PCS	NR
Hi-Opt I	L1PCS	A
Hi-Opt II	L2PCS	A
Hi-Opt Multi-Parameter	US	NR
How the Game of Blackjack is Played	PBS	NR
How to Beat Blackjack Dealers	BPS	NR
Instant Blackjack Answers Wheel	BPS	NR
Kalinevitch Ten Count	TCS	NR
Las Vegas System	L1PCS	NR
Magic Wheel of Blackjack	BPS	NR
Mayer Count System	L1PCS	NR
McGhee Plus-Minus System	L1PCS	NR
Method for Blackjack	PBS	NR
Mini Blackjack	L1PCS	NR
Money-Making Blackjack	PBS	NR
Morgan Method	BPS	NR
New Keys to Winning at Blackjack	BPS	NR
Noir One-Two Count	TCS	NR
No Need to Count	NCS	NR
Play 21 Every Day and Win	PBS	NR
PLM Money Management	PBS	NR

System	Type	Rating
Reppert Blackjack System	L2PCS	NR
R & T Complete Point-Count Strategy	L2PCS	A
Revere Five-Count Strategy	RCS	NR
Revere Ten-Count System	TCS	NR
Revere Plus-Minus Strategy	L1PCS	NR
Revere Advanced Plus-Minus	L1PCS	NR
Revere Point-Count Strategy	L2PCS	NR
Revere APC 1971	L3PCS	NR
Revere APC 1973	L3PCS	A
Roberts Ace-Count System	RCS	NR
Roberts Five-Six Count System	RCS	NR
Roberts Ten-Count System	TCS	NR
Roberts One-Number Register	L1PCS	NR
Rouge et Noir System	L1PCS	NR
Situation and Sequence	NCS	NR
Sklansky Key Card Concept	US	NR
Skovand Single-Column System	L1PCS	NR
Super Method	PBS	NR
Texas Blackjack System	PBS	NR
The Facts of Blackjack (Nolan, Walter I.)	BPS	A
The Other Man's Game (Blackjack)	PBS	NR
Thorp Five-Count System	RCS	NR
Thorp Ten-Count System	TCS	NR
Thorp Complete Point-Count	L1PCS	NR
Thorp Ultimate Strategy	US	NR
Tri-Level Blackjack	PBS	NR
Turfwin Blackjack System	PBS	NR
Ultimate Blackjack System	L1PCS	NR

System	Type	Rating
Uston Ace-Five Count	RCS	NR
Uston Advanced Plus-Minus	L1PCS	A
Uston Advanced Point-Count	L3PCS	A
Watson Sum-Plus-One Count	L3PCS	NR
Wilson Point-Count	TCS	NR
Win at Blackjack (Grant, M.)	L1PCS	NR
Win at Casino Blackjack (Jones, B.)	PBS	NR
Winning at Casino Gambling	PBS	NR
Winning Blackjack (Young, W.)	PBS	NR
Winning Blackjack Simplified	BPS	NR
Winning Gambler's Pocket Computer	BPS	NR
W. W. System	PBS	NR
Wong Halves	L3PCS	R
Wong High-Low	L1PCS	R
Z System (Bennett, L.)	BPS	NR

Information Request Form

1. THE BLACKJACK CLINIC
   Please send a brochure including pricing information and a schedule of classes for ☐

   _____
   (please specify area)

2. THE ADVANCED BLACKJACK CLINIC
   Please send pricing information and a schedule of classes. ☐

3. BLACKJACK CORRESPONDENCE COURSE
   Please send me information. ☐

4. BLACKJACK CLINIC FRANCHISE
   Please send me information on how I
   may establish a BLACKJACK CLINIC
   franchise.   ☐

5. COMPUTER-ASSISTED BLACKJACK
   TUTOR
   Please send me information.   ☐

6. ATLANTIC CITY UPDATE
   As this book goes to press there is a
   great deal of speculation about possible
   rule changes. Please send me a free
   update of the strategies and recommendations in this book that are
   changed because of new rules.   ☐

7. BLACKJACK and CASINO GAMES
   LECTURES
   Please send me information about your
   lectures service.   ☐

8. Personal Consultation.   ☐

To receive more information about The Blackjack Clinic,
please make a copy of this form, fill it out, and mail to:

   Jerry L. Patterson's Blackjack Clinic
   One Britton Place (16HB)
   Voorhees, NJ 98043
   or call (609) 772-2721

JERRY L. PATTERSON'S
Blackjack Clinic

LOCATIONS OF COURSES

Jerry L. Patterson's BLACKJACK CLINIC is offered in the following regions:

1. Mid-Atlantic Region
Classes are offered in the Greater Philadelphia area; New Jersey; Pennsylvania; Delaware; Baltimore; Washington; and in Virginia and the Carolinas.

Address: THE BLACKJACK CLINIC
One Britton Place
Voorhees, NJ 08043

Phone: (609) 772-2721

Contact: Nancy Patterson or Pam Huss

2. Northeast Region

Classes are offered in the Greater New York City area including Manhattan; Long Island; Westchester and Rockland counties; and all of New England.

Address: THE BLACKJACK CLINIC
            10 Arbor Lane
            Bardonia, NY 10954
Phone: (914) 623-0661 or (212) 410-3508
Contact: Don Schlesinger or Kenny Feldman

3. Southwest Region

Classes are offered in the Greater Los Angeles area; Central and Southern California; Nevada; Arizona; and New Mexico.

Address: 8726D South Sepulveda Blvd.
            Suite BJ-21
            Los Angeles, CA 90045
Phone: (213) 670-3683
Contact: Bob Francis or Sylvia Berger

Note: The Northwest, Central and Southeast Regions are being organized as this book goes to press. Franchises are available in all regions.

About the Author

Jerry L. Patterson is a syndicated casino-gaming columnist and the author of the popular *Blackjack's Winning Formula*. His casino-gaming column appears weekly in the *Philadelphia Bulletin*, the *Trentonian*, and monthly in the *Boardwalker Magazine*. It has also been published in the *New York Daily News*, the *San Francisco Chronicle*, the *Philadelphia Inquirer*, the *Baltimore Sun*, the *South Jersey Courier Post*, the *Asbury Park Press*, the Orange County *Register*, and the *Atlantic City Press*.

Mr. Patterson is an instructor of winning blackjack methods and founder and operator of THE BLACK-JACK CLINIC—a blackjack school that has instructed over two thousand students in *Blackjack's Winning Formula* in its first three years of operation. He is an active professional blackjack player, playing and winning in casinos all over the world.

His background as a computer scientist serves him well in the world of professional blackjack. Mr. Patterson developed a blackjack computer model with Will Cantey— one of the four developers of the original basic strategy.

Mr. Patterson has spoken out in behalf of the occasional gambler on dozens of radio and television talk shows and television news programs.

Information Request Form

1. THE BLACKJACK CLINIC
   Please send a brochure including pricing information and a schedule of
   classes for   ☐

   _____

   (please specify area)

2. THE ADVANCED BLACKJACK
   CLINIC
   Please send pricing information and a
   schedule of classes.   ☐

3. BLACKJACK CORRESPONDENCE
   COURSE
   Please send me information   ☐

4. BLACKJACK CLINIC FRANCHISE
Please send me information on how I
may establish a BLACKJACK CLINIC
franchise. ☐

5. COMPUTER-ASSISTED BLACKJACK
TUTOR
Please send me information. ☐

6. ATLANTIC CITY UPDATE
As this book goes to press there is a
great deal of speculation about possible
rule changes. Please send me a free
update of the strategies and recommendations in this book that are
changed because of new rules. ☐

7. BLACKJACK and CASINO GAMES
LECTURES
Please send me information about your
lectures service. ☐

8. Personal Consultation. ☐

To receive more information about The Blackjack Clinic,
please make a copy of this form, fill it out, and mail to:

Jerry L. Patterson's Blackjack Clinic
One Britton Place (16HB)
Voorhees, NJ 98043
or call (609) 772-2721

Information Request Form

1. THE BLACKJACK CLINIC
   Please send a brochure including pricing information and a schedule of classes for ☐

   _____
   (please specify area)

2. THE ADVANCED BLACKJACK CLINIC
   Please send pricing information and a schedule of classes. ☐

3. BLACKJACK CORRESPONDENCE COURSE
   Please send me information. ☐

4. BLACKJACK CLINIC FRANCHISE
   Please send me information on how I
   may establish a BLACKJACK CLINIC
   franchise. ☐

5. COMPUTER-ASSISTED BLACKJACK
   TUTOR
   Please send me information. ☐

6. ATLANTIC CITY UPDATE
   As this book goes to press there is a
   great deal of speculation about possible
   rule changes. Please send me a free
   update of the strategies and recommendations in this book that are
   changed because of new rules. ☐

7. BLACKJACK and CASINO GAMES
   LECTURES
   Please send me information about your
   lectures service. ☐

8. Personal Consultation. ☐

To receive more information about The Blackjack Clinic,
please make a copy of this form, fill it out, and mail to:

Jerry L. Patterson's Blackjack Clinic
One Britton Place (16HB)
Voorhees, NJ 98043
or call (609) 772-2721

Information Request Form

1. THE BLACKJACK CLINIC
   Please send a brochure including pricing information and a schedule of classes for ☐

   _____
   (please specify area)

2. THE ADVANCED BLACKJACK CLINIC
   Please send pricing information and a schedule of classes. ☐

3. BLACKJACK CORRESPONDENCE COURSE
   Please send me information. ☐

4. BLACKJACK CLINIC FRANCHISE
   Please send me information on how I
   may establish a BLACKJACK CLINIC
   franchise.   ☐

5. COMPUTER-ASSISTED BLACKJACK
   TUTOR
   Please send me information.   ☐

6. ATLANTIC CITY UPDATE
   As this book goes to press there is a
   great deal of speculation about possible
   rule changes. Please send me a free
   update of the strategies and recommendations in this book that are
   changed because of new rules.   ☐

7. BLACKJACK and CASINO GAMES
   LECTURES
   Please send me information about your
   lectures service.   ☐

8. Personal Consultation.   ☐

To receive more information about The Blackjack Clinic,
please make a copy of this form, fill it out, and mail to:

Jerry L. Patterson's Blackjack Clinic
One Britton Place (16HB)
Voorhees, NJ 98043
or call (609) 772-2721

Information Request Form

1. THE BLACKJACK CLINIC
Please send a brochure including pricing information and a schedule of classes for ☐

_____
(please specify area)

2. THE ADVANCED BLACKJACK CLINIC
Please send pricing information and a schedule of classes. ☐

3. BLACKJACK CORRESPONDENCE COURSE
Please send me information. ☐

4. BLACKJACK CLINIC FRANCHISE
   Please send me information on how I
   may establish a BLACKJACK CLINIC
   franchise.   ☐

5. COMPUTER-ASSISTED BLACKJACK
   TUTOR
   Please send me information.   ☐

6. ATLANTIC CITY UPDATE
   As this book goes to press there is a
   great deal of speculation about possible
   rule changes. Please send me a free
   update of the strategies and recommendations in this book that are
   changed because of new rules.   ☐

7. BLACKJACK and CASINO GAMES
   LECTURES
   Please send me information about your
   lectures service.   ☐

8. Personal Consultation.   ☐

To receive more information about The Blackjack Clinic,
please make a copy of this form, fill it out, and mail to:

Jerry L. Patterson's Blackjack Clinic
One Britton Place (16HB)
Voorhees, NJ 98043
or call (609) 772-2721